LAUGHTER IN STORE

by

COLIN MACLEOD

Illustrated by Ken Wilkins

Colin Macleod

Published in 2020 by Colin MacLeod
with the help of Lumphanan Press
www.lumphananpress.co.uk

Illustrations by Ken Wilkins

ISBN: 978-1-5272-6358-1

Printed and bound by Imprint Digital,
Upton Pyne, Devon, UK

ACKNOWLEDGEMENTS

I would like to record my personal gratitude and thanks to the following people whose combined efforts have helped me to produce this book.

Angela Wallis for her continued typing, and ability to decipher my stories – all written in longhand – and for laughing so much as she did. This was the spur I needed to carry on, which I publicly recognise and appreciate.

Roy MacLeod for his invaluable contribution throughout and for his assistance in putting the draft stories together.

Peter Worsley, former Assistant Editor of This England and Evergreen magazines, for his proof reading and editing, and utilising his wide experience as a professional journalist and writer.

Ken Wilkins for his superb and brilliant cartoon illustrations which embellish and add so much to the stories.

And of course my friend Alan Penn for giving his recollections, humorous stories and escapades from a lifetime in retail. Also for his continued reminding that this era of supermarketing, with all its flaws, needed to be recorded for posterity!

I owe each of you a real debt of gratitude and feel that Laughter in Store will always have a place in our hearts.

FOREWORD

For millions of people, supermarkets and superstores are now virtually a way of life. For some it's because they work there, shop there or visit them on either a daily basis or perhaps twice a week. Whatever the frequency, they are undoubtedly part of most people's weekly routine. I feel it is also true to say that nowadays every one of us simply takes supermarkets for granted. It was not, of course, always that way.

There is a little controversy over it but it's my belief that the very first supermarket in the UK was opened in Earls Court in London, way back in 1951. As it happened, I was destined to work in this small, but tremendously busy, supermarket situated practically next door to the tube station, some ten years later. By then I was part of an exciting new era of supermarkets and, as the years flew past, witnessed all the innovations, changes and technological advances taking place all around me.

I remember the excitement of continually seeing the construction of large, and then even larger stores serving more and more customers. I felt privileged to be working in an environment that had everything going for it, and I gave my supermarket career total dedication and commitment. I think back about when I joined one company in particular, who owned around 40 supermarkets at the time, a number that mushroomed to well over seven hundred by the time I left over 20 years later. My working life finally caught up with me when my knees buckled, legs gave way, and I sank to the supermarket floor.

Retirement had not just beckoned, it had arrived. It had been a lifetime in supermarkets that had overflowed with unforgettable times and memories, which included tons of arduous hard work, successes and failures, drama and excitement. That apart, it was filled with countless hilarious, and sometimes hair-raising, moments in a supermarket environment that is normally shielded from the eyes and ears of the shopping public and outsiders.

A great friend of mine, Alan Penn, has also given me a number of stories from his life in supermarkets and shops that he too has managed. This has added to the rich tapestry of true retailing life experiences in this book – hilarious, serious, and indeed dramatic, that we both shared in a period of almost 40 and 30 years respectively. Even now, looking back, we can hardly believe we have survived it all!

It therefore gives me great pleasure to re-live and share these memories and times with you.

Colin MacLeod, Summer 2020

STARTING WITH A BANG!

"Hello there!" was the greeting from the store manager, Mr. Bull, as I reached the supermarket front entrance. "I expected you earlier," he continued, adding meaningfully, "I've been here since 7 a.m." I replied "You never mentioned my actual starting time at the interview – only the store's opening hours, and that I should be early." He cut me off abruptly and, after staring at me continued "I must say, I didn't remember you being so small. Could be a slight problem – we've only got a size 44 male white overall." My mind was already racing. Slight problem? I was only five foot two and a half inches, nine stone and wiry. "Jess, take this chap … er Colin, to the staff room and get the size 44 overall in the cupboard, make it fit him – use safety pins or something but get him kitted out." He asked me to come to his office when I was ready for action.

In the small staff room I was soon enveloped in this huge overall, surrounded by Jess and another girl called Moira. "We'll take the hem up and use these safety pins. They're all we've got." They proceeded with this impossible task and I could see the hem was going to be about 18 inches in

1

depth – and it didn't look good. They rolled the sleeves up on my arms until I felt sure there was now a circulation of blood problem. "Best we can do," was Jess's last comment, and I was on my way to Mr. Bull for the day's instructions.

I immediately realised there was also a mobility problem. When I turned my body to the right, the bulk of the overall did not follow but remained static until I wrenched it along. I was also aware of badly stifled giggles from the girls but this I had to ignore.

"Right son," barked Mr. Bull, (or the Raging Bull, as I soon realised he was called), "I want you to work on the fruit and vegetable display cabinet. Pop these potatoes from that sack in front of the scale on the far end of the fixture into the polythene bags and then put them on the bay in front. Weigh five pounds into each bag, tie the top of it, and there you are. You can use a scale, can't you?" I assured him I could, although I'd only used a scale like it helping a local shopkeeper in my school holidays. I was now 17 so no problem surely. "If," the Raging Bull concluded, "someone wants something in the way of fruit or other vegetables weighed, use the scales on the other end of the display unit. O.K. Got that?" I nodded, and turned to the waiting sack of spuds as Bull strode off.

Quite soon I realised I possessed a hitherto unknown talent for pre-packing spuds, and in no time I was setting a cracking pace, my confidence growing by the minute. "Excuse me, young man." A sweet sounding female voice suddenly sounded from the opposite end to where I was so industriously working. I looked up and a very attractive lady in her thirties was holding a small bunch of bananas in her hand opposite the scale. She smiled and continued, "Could you please weigh these and put a price on the bag?"

"Yes, certainly ma'am," I replied with enthusiasm. My moment had arrived – my first customer! I swivelled round scarcely disguising my excitement and quickly stepped forward in her direction, still clutching a polythene bag of potatoes in my right hand. On later reflection it was clear that my body had once again turned round much more quickly than my white overall, and as a result my left foot and ankle became instantly lodged in the hem of my huge overall. Subsequently I nose-dived on to the hard tiled floor, my face crashing with a sickening thud before any other part of my body. Because I was instinctively clutching the polythene bag of potatoes, my feet were not actually touching the floor. It all happened so suddenly. Dazed, I could hear voices above my head and blood was now running down my cheeks. "Stay still," one of the store girls cried. "We're trying to get your foot out!" But they couldn't, and I was suddenly aware of three pairs of arms lifting me up and carrying me from the sales floor – a bit like a stricken gladiator being removed from an ancient arena in Rome. I was propped up on a chair in the staff room whilst my foot and ankle were unpinned from the hem. A cold cloth was mercifully placed on my brow, whilst the blood was wiped away with another cloth. The cut above my eye was cleaned and a plaster applied. My nose stopped bleeding

3

and the girls were removing the offending overall. "How is he?" Mr. Bull's voice sounded from somewhere. "He'll be O.K." replied Moira, "… but he'll need to stay here for a while – he's a bit white and shaken."

I had now recovered enough to be fully aware of the situation so when Mr. Bull came into view I tore into him – first day or not. "It's all your fault. You should have had my size of overall here ready for me then this wouldn't have happened." Mr. Bull was caught off balance and in a somewhat cowed manner he replied he would make sure there was the right size overalls for me to wear the next day. There was no apology, only the follow up instruction to come to his office when I felt better. "I'm making some tea for him," said Moira, "and he's got to stay in the staff room till he feels better." Mr Bull nodded and disappeared. Moira smiled at me. She was a pretty girl …"Now drink this mug of tea and I'll change that plaster. Don't you hurry back – take your time – don't worry about the Raging Bull – he's a clown!"

I felt much better. Half an hour later I saw Mr. Bull and took the initiative. "I'm not wearing an overall or going on the shop floor today like this. What I can do – since I'm the only male here – is sort out the warehouse. The stock room is in a mess. It'll take me the rest of the day, but I'll do a good job for you – you'll see. O.K.?" Mr. Bull could do little but agree.

Sitting on a cornflakes box I had time to reflect. I'd been pleased to get the opportunity to begin a new

4

career working in Aberdeen's first brand new supermarket. Situated in the area known as Northfield, it was surrounded on all sides by council flats and houses, and even I could appreciate the store was well equipped to serve this neighbourhood. It included a fresh meat and delicatessen counter and also fresh bakery counters. There was a fine partially self-service fruit and vegetables section, a wines and spirits counter, and even a delivery service if required. There were two aisles of grocery products and I reckoned if this supermarket was efficiently managed – already in grave doubt – it could do well, and hopefully I could both learn my trade and play my part in its progress.

The warehouse was a piece of cake and I enjoyed the challenge. I was also left alone to get on with it, and by late in the afternoon was almost finished when I noticed what looked like a magazine wedged between two stacks of boxes in the corner. On the floor were some cigarette stubs and on a ledge was somebody's empty coffee or tea mug. Whose little secret corner was this? Could only have been the boss! By moving the stacks I retrieved a magazine called *Health and Efficiency* which was full of photographs of nude women, and even a few men too. "Well, well" I thought.

The warehouse complete, I went to the office, first having wrapped the magazine in some brown paper so nobody could see what it was. It proved to be my bargaining tool with Mr. Bull who had already seen my recent efforts and commented that I hadn't done a bad job at all.

"I'm off home now," I told him, adding, "Now you will have that overall my size for me tomorrow, won't you?" Before he could reply, I added, "Oh, yes. Found this in the warehouse and thought I'd keep it from the staff." He opened the brown package and found his magazine. "Yes" he replied without a trace of emotion. I reminded him, once again, that he needed to have my correct-sized overall ready the following morning. "Don't worry," he replied. "I'm collecting it from our other shop tonight."

It had been quite a first day in the world of supermarkets and there was much more fun and games waiting around the corner!

WE ALL MAKE MISTAKES

As manager of a North London supermarket in the 1960s, I was summoned to the checkout to attend to an apparently irate customer with a serious complaint. She rounded on me the moment she saw me, thrusting a red plastic-coated large continental sausage into my hands, yelling "I bought this here – just look at the code date – you should be prosecuted for selling it. It's a perfect disgrace!" By this time I was aware of around a dozen pairs of eyes belonging to those queuing, now focused on me. She continued her tirade concluding with "Well, what have you got to say?" Meanwhile, I was examining the sausage thoroughly and could scarcely believe my eyes – and my luck. "Only this, Madam" I replied slowly, deliberately and clearly. "You did not buy this here – I know this because of the other label on it. We are always very careful about codes as our customers know. Look there and you will see for yourself!" I handed it back to her. "Oh dear, oh dear, you are right – I'm sorry I blamed you for this." To save her further embarrassment, I said with a smile, "It's alright – we all make mistakes." The queuing faces were smiling by now and suddenly, as soon as

7

she had departed, a lady rushed forward and gave me a kiss and a hug, adding meaningfully with a smile "I can't stand that horrible woman – I wouldn't have missed this for the world!" Looking back, I wish every complaint had been that easy to deal with.

CUSTOMER COMPLAINTS
I REMEMBER

"I just pierced this can to get the tomatoes out and the juice inside shot out like a fireman's hose and it went everywhere! The kitchen walls, sink, table, floor … looked like they'd been painted red!" Before, as Manager, I could respond, he continued in a matter-of-fact gentle way to describe what happened next … "I had just cleaned my kitchen fire extinguisher on the wall. I stretched up to get it down, but dropped it, and next thing everything was covered in foam … It was everywhere!" By now my body ached from suppressed laughter and he finished his description of his kitchen disasters, saying "Well, it was just one those things. Oh, and here's the can so you can check if there any others like it." As my laughter had by now well and truly started, I asked him to follow me, which he did. "I'm not going to give you another can of tomatoes but would you like this to enjoy instead?" I presented him with a bottle of fine Scotch malt whisky. "Have this on us and I trust you'll enjoy it?" "Yes, I will" he replied. "I never expected this. I

9

just wanted to warn you about the can …" Salt of the earth this pensioner customer was – a lovely man!

LEFT HOLDING THE REINS

Unfortunately, every company has from time to time a director who is too full of his own importance and subsequently at times prone to be arrogant and rude! A past recipient of his rudeness was an invaluable member of staff at a supermarket in Hampshire's New Forest. She had been the admin clerk and chief cashier and, indeed, unofficial assistant manager there for many years. On this particular morning she noticed him walking briskly past the front window towards the entrance. However, a local character nicknamed "Colonel Chinstrap" had other ideas. "Hold on to this, will you please, my dear chap – got to pop in for my papers and tobacco – won't be two minutes." The director now found himself hanging on to the reins of a horse positioned just outside the entrance. At this precise moment the telephone rang and the admin clerk answered it, immediately recognising the CEO's voice on the line. He asked her if the director was there. "Well, he is and he isn't, she replied. "Whatever do you mean?" replied the CEO, understandably baffled. She went on to explain that she had seen him looking after a horse outside the front of

11

the store, but that she would go and arrange for him to take the call straight away." "Thank you" was the reply. "And tell him, if he sees another horse on the way, to ignore it. I want to speak to him and it's important." After passing this message on, she admitted she found it impossible to suppress a giggle as she watched the director hurry in to take the call, while she literally, you could say took over the reins. Being rude to a female is always unwise – say something by all means that has to be said, but be charming with it and you won't lose out!

KNUCKLING DOWN

I wonder how many old grocers like me ever had the task of removing adhesive cloths from the rounded sides of large whole cheeses prior to their being "wired up" into manageable portions? An unenviable job for sure. Where I worked as apprentice grocer, we called it "skinning" and when dealing with a hard crusty extra mature Canadian cheddar, and as I wrenched the cloth off the side, a lump of cheese the size of a large plum attached itself to the removed cloth. Hungry, I popped it into my mouth at the same instant the boss appeared behind me! The extra strong flavour put my taste buds into overdrive. Unable to speak, tears now rolled down my cheeks! Noticing this, the boss said, "What's the matter with you?" I winced, held up my knuckles and pointed to the cheese. To which he replied, "Don't be such a wimp. You've got two more to do … crack on."

I didn't mind at that moment what he thought of me as long as he never realised what I'd done. It was something I never ever repeated, you can be sure of that.

SPIRIT OF THE BLITZ

I'd worked the whole night through, as workmen replaced essential cables beneath parts of the supermarket floor in Earls Court High Street. However, I'd failed to notice that one of the workmen had inadvertently left the front entrance door ajar and opening time was still five minutes away. Far more importantly, the heavy, long wrought-iron cover had not been put into place yet over the eight foot long, four foot wide trench, which was also three foot deep. The workmen had, for convenience, been walking along a narrow, wobbly plank which was still in position. You can imagine my horror when I saw a frail, oldish lady pick her way carefully along it with a basket over one arm and a shopping bag on the other! I froze, whilst everyone else held their breath.

When she had safely reached the sales floor, I rushed over to apologise and explain but she simply smiled and replied, "Young man. When you have survived the Blitz and the doodle bugs, this (she pointed to the trench) was nothing! Don't worry about it at all." I raced outside to the pavement to the flower stall being set up and bought a nice bunch which I gave to her as she left. She smiled sweetly and said, "Thank you! There was no need for you to do that but thank you", and with that she gave me a little hug as she walked away. My admiration for the spirit of this London lady in the early-1960s has remained with me ever since.

OUR OLDE VILLAGE SHOP

The ringing of a shop doorbell
The jars of sweet, fantastic smells
Evoke in me a memory
Of halcyon days that used to be.

Woodbine packets on the shelf
Tobacco you could roll yourself
Craven A for those with brass and
Capstan for the upper class.

Not one shelf we had was empty
Sunlight soap we had aplenty
Hair clips, liquorish sticks and such
The locals did not want for much.

Ours was just a Parlour shop
With laxatives and home-made pop
Gravy browning, tins of stew
Packs of tea to make a brew.

Mrs Evans with her stick
Like others, got her stuff on tick.
My father lacked so much, in fact
He used to countermand this act.

My mother wasn't keen on trust
"If goods you want then pay you must"
So to my mind there is no doubt
Some customers would wait till Mum went out.

We made some money in these days
Which helped us out in many ways.
Then came the War, and then the rot
The blinkin' bombs wiped out the lot.

A BRUSH WITH THE LAW

On my first day of management at the supermarket in Sidcup High Street, Kent, I discovered the glass front entrance door had three separate locks: one at the top, middle and bottom. Trouble was, being on the short side, I could not reach the top lock! At 6am the street was empty but I spied what I thought would be the solution just three doors away – a freshly delivered bottle of milk. I sidled along to their door and stealthily borrowed it – just for a couple of minutes I thought. I placed it at the foot of the door and was just about to step on top of it when the words "Ello, ello, ello!" assailed my ears. "And what do you think you're doing?"

I turned round to find myself staring up at a policeman who'd spotted me while doing his early morning beat. He had a twinkle in his eye and, after a quick explanation, he said "You go and put the bottle back and I'll open the door for you!" This I duly did, and offered him a cuppa. He could not stop but said he'd pop in soon to see how I was settling in later in the week.

Putting this embarrassing moment aside, the fact is, Sidcup was my happiest managerial assignment ever!

TOM AND JERRY, IN REAL LIFE

As I alighted from the bus outside the supermarket in Grove Park, London, where I'd been detailed to do a relief managerial stint, I noticed a several people gazing intently through the store's front window. I was shocked when I saw the reason why! On top of a tightly packed five foot high by four feet long stack of granulated sugar, was a mouse, running from side to side, and on the floor at the base of the stack was a menacing cat – clearly frustrated at not being able to get at the mouse! Enough was enough, and I opened the front door just as both entertainers disappeared. From the watchers I received a chorus of ooohs and aahs and somebody even called out "spoilsport." It transpired the store had a mice problem and somebody had engaged a cat to patrol the warehouse above the sales floor over the weekend but obviously the chase had continued out to the sugar stack.

Fortunately for me the company's vermin control specialist soon arrived. Problem solved and the cat was redundant!

THE FLYING HAGGIS!

After weighing and pricing umpteen polythene bags filled with potatoes, and running the fruit and vegetables display counter, I was ordered one morning in an emergency to serve and run the counter which displayed fresh and cooked meats, sliced bacon, cheeses and lines like black puddings. Unfortunately, I'd been given no training and the first customer selected a plump round haggis which I duly weighed, slid into a brown paper bag, and then put a price ticket on it. Without thinking, I gripped the top corners of the bag between the fingers of each hand and twirled it around, thinking to keep the contents safe. To my horror the haggis shot out of the bottom like a cannonball, narrowly missing the startled lady's head and crashing into the cans on the shelf behind her. The boss arrived instantly and, just as he began to berate me, the lady looked at him calmly and said, "It was only an accident. No harm done, and it is good to see somebody pleasant behind the counter, unlike the girl before." The boss sloped off as I apologised to her, after which I selected an alternative haggis and this time served her safely.

SEARCHING FOR A CAN
WITH A PROBLEM

"I got quite a shock when I saw it in the can!" said this customer, and handed me a large can of South African peach halves in heavy syrup to inspect. Embedded in a peach was half of the largest bumblebee I'd ever seen. "I always buy this brand", he continued, "because the quality is so good, so a replacement tin will be fine." This occurred in the days when such an action was sufficient for the customer, so I apologised for the inconvenience he'd had and replaced the can.

He later returned with the same can. Incredibly, the other half of the insect was in it's contents! I filled in a customer complaint form which included his name and address, refunded him with cash and told him I'd write to the company on his behalf and send on the insect evidence. Some weeks later he came to see me in my office. This time, highly delighted! "The company who produced the cans of peaches sent me a letter of apology and also included a large box full of samples – yum, yum!" He smiled broadly adding,

"Thank you for your trouble and writing to them. I'm off now to buy some more cans of their peaches – keeping my fingers crossed I get another one with something in it that shouldn't be there. Can I be that lucky again?" He didn't find such a can but it seemed he had definitely developed a taste for that particular company's products!!

CLEANING MISHAP

As I passed the front windows of a small supermarket near me, I noticed the window cleaner cleaning the fascia letters on it with a dripping wet cloth perched on the end of a pole.

I smiled as I recollected the occasion when I felt compelled to use this same method myself in an impulsive moment when I was a manager. Unfortunately, in my case, the soaking wet cloth decided to come off at the very moment a retired male customer carrying his groceries was exiting the store. I shouted in utter horror "Look out!" but it was too late and the cloth – still soaking – landed plum on top of his shiny head! I hung my head in shame and tried to apologise but he would have none of it. "Listen," he replied, after removing the offending cloth. "I'm relieved! I thought it was the droppings from one of those seagulls up there – now that would not have been very funny." Thankfully he was a regular customer with a great sense of humour, otherwise it could have been a tricky moment!

BAGS OF TROUBLE!

Frustratingly for all, the order placed for large and medium-sized bags for use at the tills had not been honoured by the supply depot. This placed the cashiers in a difficult situation, albeit temporary. However, one male customer in a foul mood, vented his fury at the till operator when he tried to pack his shopping. "Are these small bags all you've got?" he said loudly, adding "This is ridiculous. Is there nothing on this till bigger than these bags?" The cashier had had enough and she responded with "Yes there is. Your mouth!" The queuing customers all laughed! Of course she shouldn't have said it but the customer was manly enough to apologise to her. "Sorry, Luv," he said "I'm just having a bad morning, but it's no good me taking it out on you – not your fault. I'll manage." "Don't worry about paying – and I'm sorry I said that too" replied the cashier. "I hope your day improves!"

THE FUNNY SIDE

After shopping at my local new Co-op supermarket at Beauly in Scotland, I turned left as usual in the direction of my car, only to see a gentleman staring at the first trolley in the third row, furthest from the entrance. I noticed the trolley move slightly. "Stay there," he said suddenly. "Stay, and don't you move!" I stood there looking at him and found myself saying, "You're speaking to that trolley like a dog." He turned round and looked at me and replied, "I am speaking to a dog – it's behind the end trolley. You thought I was off my trolley, didn't you!"

At this we both enjoyed a good laugh – just what we needed at 8.45 am on a rainy morning!

ACCIDENTAL HERO

"He'll do a runner, for sure" said the female security officer to me after she'd spotted a man well over six feet in height, shoplifting. "Get somebody to help you and stand outside the door, out of sight, and be ready!" were her instructions.

She stopped him on the pavement outside the shop. I was taken aback at the physique of the giant, as was the overweight butcher beside me, who I'd asked to help me. Bad choice. The security officer gave me a glance just as the apprehended shoplifter started to flee the scene. I took off in pursuit leaving the portly butcher on the starting blocks. The shoplifter's long legs began to take huge strides as he ran, in contrast to my short legs, which were going like pistons. Quite accidentally my foot caught the back of his right ankle and down he fell with an almighty clatter. Without hesitation I dived on top of him, but realised in a fraction of a second, he was far too strong for me. I am grateful to this day to an equally large gentleman who was passing, one of our customers who, without hesitation, put his knee on the shoplifter's chest and pinned him down. Surrounded by passers by we were soon attended too by a local constable from the police station across the road. Once again I knew I'd been a lucky boy.

The company's weekly bulletin sent to all company stores reported this incident and were too kind to me – "The mighty atom strikes again !" it boomed out! (If only that was really true!)

PUSHING TOO HARD

"That's not how to brush a shop floor!" I said sharply to a young chap who had only just been taken on, so I grabbed the brush and got down on one knee, indicating he did the same. "See that bit of floor you think you've brushed? It should have a gleam but hasn't!" then added "I'll brush over the area you've done and I'll have a bigger pile of dust than you." I was just finishing my demonstration and already he could see my pile of dirt was much larger and he'd supposedly brushed the area before me! "Look!" I said loudly, "You have got to put your back into it and push the brush hard into the floor!" I decided to demonstrate what I meant so I pushed extra hard on the brush but the handle broke and I fell forward right into the pile of dust I'd collected. As I lay there I looked up at the young lad who had a startled look on his face. "It's OK" I said, "You can laugh, I know it's funny and so do you!" He smiled, then laughed. "You won't forget this demonstration will you?" I said, "… but you now know how hard I like you to push the brush." He nodded but only just stopped himself laughing. I couldn't blame him.

PRIDE COMES BEFORE A MISHAP!

An unexpected midday visit from an unpopular senior director is never welcomed by managers, so when one arrived and without ado started walking around the sales floor, clearly looking for anything he could criticise, it wasn't the best thing to suffer. In his dark, pinstripe suit, white shirt and smart tie, he stopped at the dairy cabinet. It had been filled but was showing tell tale signs of a busy two hours trading. His eyes focused on a large pot of yogurt that had been placed slightly away from it's normal location and said "I like to see my stores tidy. Now that is what I don't like to see – something sitting where it shouldn't." So saying, and in some irritation, he stretched out and grabbed the large pot. What neither of us knew was that some customer had dropped it on the floor and, despite its split sides, had put the pot where he had found it. In a split second the contents spilled out – all down his shirt, jacket and trousers. "Oh dear," I explained, "some customer ...." "Never mind that – look at my clothes ..." "Follow me to the staff room" I replied "and we'll soon get your clothes smartened up – in privacy."

31

He grunted and followed me. After plenty of hot water and household towels I'd cleaned him up. OK there were temporary signs of dampness – even wetness – but the job was done. "I've lost more than enough time with this happening, so I'm going" he said curtly. "If the office phones they'll know where I'll be", and with that he took his leave. "It couldn't have worked out better or to a nicer chap" I remarked to my assistant manager, who was grinning from ear to ear.

A SMILE GOES A LONG WAY

Only a few days after starting at my new store I was constructing a display on the sales floor which involved stacking tray after tray to a height of nearly six feet. I was surrounded by whole cases of cans and, being short of stature, was standing on a case to enable me to position the final tray. A passing customer who could only see the upper part of my body, asked me where an item was in the store. I alighted from the box and walked towards her. She met me with a deprecating "Oh, I never realised you were so small!""You are so personal and rude" I cried in mock anger. However, lacking a sense of humour, she was startled. "Oh I am sorry" she blurted out apologetically. I didn't mean to be ...". I smiled broadly, "Only joking my dear, only joking ..." Now she broke into a wide smile – clearly relieved. "I think what you want is right here" I said, and handed her what she wanted. As she walked off, a member of staff came across to me and exclaimed "In all the years I've worked here, that miserable old bat has never once smiled. Don't know how you did it – so that's a first I can tell you!" I saw her quite a few more times afterwards and she always gave me a smile! I was clearly special!

THE DELIVERY MAN AIRS HIS VIEWS

At one store there was a loudspeaker system at the back door reception area. The tannoy itself was on an expanding metal flex and normally was clipped on to a hook. The young back door man was under pressure as he helped unload and check a lorry load when another lorry driver appeared. He used the tannoy to call for someone to report to the back door to help him but no one came. "Wait a minute" he said to the driver. "I'm going to get somebody to help." Unfortunately he left the button on the tannoy down, so all the voices could be heard everywhere, plus help was taking longer to arrive. The drivers were understandably fed up and suddenly over the sales floor came an expletive-strewn conversation. Sadly, the drivers were unaware their conversation was being broadcast right across the store! I rushed to rectify the problem but when I returned to the sales area, one or two customers were looking at me with raised eyebrows. "Sorry, ladies" I said, "but at least you now know what we have to put up with just to get the food lines in through the back door!" I shook my head, while they had a chuckle.

THE FATE OF THE VISITING CHAIRMAN

The company's chairman was expected. I was managing our Oxford store and all the staff were there for the 10am deadline, all spick and span. Anticipation was high. The front of the store was on the High Street and to park one had to turn left and left again then find the entrance to a covered enclosed area. This back door reception area, however, also used by two other stores. The gold Rolls Royce was spotted passing the window and word was immediately passed around. We waited and waited, but surprisingly no one appeared. After ten minutes I decided to open the back door to see where the Rolls had parked but there was no sign of it! The chauffeur, I'd been previously advised, knew where our rear door was but both the chairman and the Rolls were conspicuous by their absence.

A phone call then came through and I had to promise not to reveal what I was told to anyone. Apparently, the chairman had seen what he thought was our back door both wide open and unattended. We would obviously have been reprimanded if caught out like this. He then wandered inside, past boxes and stock strewn apparently everywhere – a right mess. When the shopkeeper made an appearance the chairman began to indicate his displeasure at what he'd found. The big Polish owner of the health food shop whose warehouse the chairman had unwittingly found himself in, was not at all amused and grabbed the diminutive chairman by his lapels and bodily lifted him outside and threw him down amongst some empty cardboard and rubbish, accompanied by a ferocious "Get out and stay out!". The chairman promptly picked himself up, got into the Rolls, and ordered the chauffeur to drive away as fast as he could. I was instructed to inform the staff that he'd been urgently called away on business. I agreed but asked if a director could pop down to make a visit and praise the staff who had worked so hard. It was quickly agreed but we never did see the Chairman!

ALL IN A DAY'S WORK

One tricky moment I recall from my Oxford manager's days, occurred when a most attractive, slim lady was shopping in the main aisle. As I walked towards her I noticed her suddenly stop, stiffen and stand quite straight. As she stepped forward gingerly, a pair of pink almost see-through panties, slipped slowly down to her ankles. Cool as a cucumber she stepped out of them and simply carried on! There was nobody else about to witness what had happened, so without comment, or giving her a glance, I picked them up and selected a small brown paper bag from one of the checkouts, popped them in unnoticed, and walked back to the lady who was continuing shopping.

Her large shopping bag was draped over her arm and, as I passed her, I deftly pushed the paper bag into it. She turned round and gave me a quick Mona Lisa-like smile and a quick nod. Interestingly, I never saw her again in the store!

WEARING A THICK COAT
ON A HOT DAY?

"Fancy wearing a long thick coat on a hot day like this," said one of my female staff as she pointed a customer out. As I watched him for a few seconds he seemed just a little bit nervous, quickly glancing left and right. It was amusing for only a moment or two until the penny dropped. "He's a shoplifter" I whispered to the assistant. "Watch him, but keep out of sight if you can. I'll do the same." We were successful. As it turned out he was dropping small but expensive items into large, long pockets. My assistant confirmed this and we stopped him outside and brought him back to the office.

We asked him to empty his pockets and he'd nicked quite a haul so we called the local police. As I waited I couldn't resist remarking, "Hot day for a coat like that – and it's ... er ... getting even hotter!" As she left the office I heard my assistant give a little chuckle but our offender was now feeling the heat. Looking at what he'd tried to pinch, I reckoned I'd be the same!

39

COMPANY CARS ARE MORE VERSATILE

If you were a manager at certain stores the huge bonus of a company car was part of the financial package. I was lucky to have this just once and when I was on holiday a special meeting was called at head office to be attended by all who had company cars. My understanding was that it was to be a pep talk about looking after its condition and not in any way abusing what was seen as a special perk. I asked a colleague on my return from holiday if he'd tell me what was covered at the meeting. I should have remembered he had a particularly quirky sense of humour, though when his note came through in the post to me I could not help laughing guiltily.

Company Cars
1.   Travel faster in all gears, especially reverse.
2.   Accelerate at a phenomenal rate.
3.   Enjoy a much shorter braking distance.
4.   They have a much tighter turning circle.

5. They can take ramps at twice the speed of private cars.

6. Battery, water, oil and tyre pressure are not required to be checked so often.

7. Use only the petrol with the best garage incentives.

8. They do not require to be garaged at night.

9. They can be driven for up to 100 miles with the oil warning light flashing.

10. They need cleaning less often.

11. The suspension is reinforced to allow carriage of concrete slabs and other heavy building materials.

12. They are adapted to allow reverse gear to be engaged while the car is still moving forward.

13. The tyre walls are designed to allow bumping into and over kerbstones.

14. Unusual and alarming engine noises are easily eliminated by the adjustment of the fitted radio volume control.

15. No security needed. May be left anywhere, unlocked with the keys in the ignition.

As I read his missive I had to admit there were some points I'd do well to remember!

A MANAGERIAL HERO

A pal of mine was manager of a particularly difficult super-market in Berkshire. As all managers know only too well, a combination of absenteeism (often for acceptable reasons) and a temporary problem in replacing key staff who have left, makes life at times very hard. If support from within the company is not forthcoming, any manager will tell you that coping with this temporary situation is all you can do until it ultimately improves.

A young executive from Bristol head office, known for his brash, arrogant approach – borne out of too little experience – arrived unexpectedly. He was not happy and demanded the busy overworked manager accompany him on a tour of the store. He was soon, in his ignorant style, getting on the manager's back and throwing the odd wobbly. As they completed their walk around he stopped suddenly and said quite loudly, "You know I've been think-ing" – and he paused here for dramatic effect – "I wouldn't personally do my shopping at your store. I really wouldn't!" "Well," drawled the manager (now thoroughly fed up), "that's very understandable and a jolly good idea – it's a blinkin' long way to come from Bristol, just to do your shopping!"

It is said that you could hear the executive's teeth grinding in the next aisle!' I never did hear the final outcome of his visit but am certain he never did any shopping there!

JOB APPLICANTS CAN BE FUNNY!

Born with a sense of humour and a tendency to laugh out loud when somebody says something funny, was something I had to curb at times, especially if I had to interview people looking for a job, especially those unsuited for a career in the mad supermarket environment. Some examples come to mind:

Watching a middle aged burly man filling in the application form, I confess I looked over his shoulder at what he was writing. In the slot that asked "Name of previous employer and your job", he'd written "Elephant Trainer, Chipperfields Circus. That was for the last three years." "What did you do before that?" I asked. He looked at me, shrugged and wrote, "Elephant Trainer, Bertram Mills Circus." This time he'd been even longer there. "I'm afraid we need someone with grocery or shop experience, at least," I explained, "and your experience would not help you here. Elephants never forget – it's the opposite with staff here, sorry to say. Sorry we can't fit you in but good luck in finding something." He took it in good spirit, smiled, shrugged and trudged off.

I was intrigued when I read on one application the "Reason for leaving." The young girl had written, "Automatic dustbin." I enquired why. "When you got rid of your rubbish," she explained, "You had to take it outside to a large bin. You then had to press your foot down on a pedal and keep it there. The lid would lift up but the moment you took your foot off the pedal it came crashing down. Well, I couldn't get this to work for me and in the end got tired of the lid hitting my head or fingers. And told them so – and left – wouldn't you?" I found myself saying, "Our system is the same! Technical things like this aren't for you!" The interview was terminated.

45

One butcher I interviewed listed his last four employers and his reasons for leaving. The first was "Left after row with the management." The next was "Due to aggravation received from the management." The reason for leaving his last two jobs hardly came as a surprise: "Unable to work with manager and disagreement with management."

I stared at the application while he had a bullish look about him and was aware of his eyes staring at me intently. In the ensuing silence there was a growing tension. Looking straight at him, I took the bull by the horns, and said quietly, "Reading this, and why you left your last four shops, it seems to me that you have a clear problem with management. Would you think, on reflection, that you might have been too aggressive at times when you disagreed with what they wanted?" At this he rose from his seat slowly, the palms of his hands pushing down on the table whilst he leaned forward towards me and rasped, "What do you mean aggressive? I'm not aggressive. It wasn't me that was aggressive – it was them. Every time!" Still staring at me he picked up the application form, slowly crushed it into a ball and chucked it in the direction of the waste paper bin. I received a contemptuous stare before he stomped off and recall thinking he sorely needed some anger management before attempting to work alongside any supermarket manager! Perhaps self-employment was his answer!

CHARLIE SORTED IT OUT!

"Whatever's the matter, Margie?" I anxiously asked one of my female staff when she arrived for work at a South London supermarket. "I've been burgled – they took my record player, cassette player, records and cassettes, spare cash in a drawer and some other items. Turned my flat over, they did." she replied.

"This just isn't acceptable", I said angrily. "Take time off now and go to the police and report it. Don't worry about work – I'll get your work covered – you go on and see what can be done."

"I'm not going to the police", Margie replied, in an extremely positive voice. "But Margie …" I started, but she cut me off. "I'm going to see Charlie – he'll sort it out for me." "Charlie?" I replied. She responded quickly. "Charlie Richardson, a well known London gang leader who was in my class at school. I know Charlie ..."

Next morning Margie returned to work but this time with a smile on her face. "Well," I greeted her, "How did you get on?" "Charlie sorted it, as I said he would. Got it all back for me … and a lot more!"

I knew Margie well and confess I now felt very safe managing a supermarket in Charlie's manor. A funny feeling but that's the truth of it.

FAINTING OVER A FINGER!

Managing a supermarket on the South Coast of England, I recall two related quirky incidents. The fresh meat counter was a popular feature and the butchers' displays were always beautifully presented. There was a block at the back of the counter against a tiled wall where they boned the meat, serving it up when required. One of the butchers was a bit of a joker but not all of his pranks were appreciated, either by customers or indeed by the staff. He was a good butcher but a potential liability.

One busy morning his partner was slicing some meat on the block when he suddenly exclaimed and cursed the fact that he'd cut his finger. For a couple of moments he held his hand and bent double, something not missed by the queuing customers. His fellow butcher, (the joker) unseen, grabbed a small skinless sausage from a tray and pretended to pick it up from the floor. "Don't worry, don't worry," he said loudly looking at the customers. "I've found it," pretending to refer to his colleague's finger and held it in the palm of his hand, adding "We'll soon get it sewn back on." It was a joke in poor taste and one lady customer in the queue swayed and clutched at the lady next to her before fainting! She came round quickly and thankfully the butcher apologised and showed her the finger was only a sausage. Two of the girls took her to the staff room and revived her with a cup of tea. The other butcher had, meantime, put a piece of cloth on his finger. He then announced the cut needed cleaning and bandaging and made his way to my office. The cut was a clean one and I went to the first aid box to put some antiseptic ointment on and started to bandage it. The butcher, however, was suffering and could neither look at his finger nor at my first aid effort.

All went well until I needed a pair of scissors but there was not one to hand so I thought a knife would do. Forgetting the butcher was watching, I said innocently, looking at the bandage excess, "I'm afraid I'm going to have to use the knife in the drawer to cut it off." Already in panic mode and somehow believing I was now going to cut his finger off, he grabbed at the desk before slowly sinking to the floor in a faint!! I reassured him all was OK and he recovered his composure.

What a day!

51

NICKING – OR KNICKERING?

In my early days I had the task of making up polythene bags of potatoes for the greengrocery department which had a sloping series of mirrors. The large bag of potatoes was placed near a scale on the display unit and the boss said "If any customer comes to the other scale and wants you to weigh and price what they have selected (bananas cherries, etc.) – do it and put the price on the bag. One morning I spilled some potatoes which rolled under the nearby grocery fixtures so I got down on my hands and knees to collect them but as I got up something reflected in the mirrors caught my eye. A woman was shoplifting in the next aisle. She was incredibly shoving groceries into her old fashioned, Directoire knickers! As a young lad I could hardly believe my eyes but seeing was believing.

I went to the boss's office and told him and, with a female member of staff, he apprehended the shoplifter after she had left the store and called the police. When she had departed the scene with the law, I went to see the boss and on his desk were the stolen items, including wrapped bacon, cheese and meats. "Put them all back – we have the details so that's OK. Go on then!" he barked. He might have had no scruples nor proper respect for his customers but I had. I put the goods in a box and, out of sight of everyone, I went to the back door and deposited them smartly into one of the bins. He never knew what I did but my little respect for him was confirmed when he was fired for poor management within months.

THERE IT WAS . . . GONE!

The second London store where I was asked to be assistant manager was in Edgware. The supermarket had originally been a Woolworths store with its wooden floor still in place. I opened up one morning and realised something was not right. In fact, something was missing! Our long frozen food cabinet had been leaking water for a while and its insulation was highly suspect and due for replacement. Our wooden floor had actually succumbed to the regular dripping and the refrigerator had simply sunk through its saturated wooden base and dropped into the store's foundations.

Time for action. The frozen foods had already defrosted and were quickly removed. Meantime, I covered the long hole with the sides of cages used to hold grocery lines, got some flattened cardboard laid over the top to cover the hole, and had some temporary "Keep Off" display cards printed plus a couple of cards simply stating that a new freezer was on the way to replace the old one – "Sorry for any temporary inconvenience!"

My action met with the boss's approval – when he

arrived! – and head office moved quickly in getting a replacement freezer. That's the thing about supermarkets – every day is different!

THE POWER OF EXTRA STRONG MINTS!

I get a Christmas card every year from a former member of staff who says Christmas Eve is a time when her thoughts go back to extra strong mints!

The female members of staff used to traditionally go out to a nearby pub for a couple of gin and tonics and, although it was against company policy, I just hadn't the heart to stop them. Trouble was, it was at lunchtime when they went – not the end of the day. The company had a female security officer who was eagle-eyed and I suspected that if she knew, it would be reported to head office with trouble for one and all. She, sadly, would not have cared one little bit so I used to buy stacks of extra strong mints and demanded, when they returned from the pub, that they all ate them non-stop to prevent their breath giving them away. I also used to dash round the store checking all afternoon!

It was a successful ploy, and, although a bit hair-raising, it worked every time with one member still sending me an

annual card which includes best wishes from all those who
were the recipients of those extra strong mints!

NO PAPER, NO PEN,
BUT NO PROBLEMS!

Strolling along Wardour Street in Soho in London in 1965 on my way to the Bank, I met David Frost. Only the previous evening I had watched *That Was The Week That Was* on TV. His name was already known to millions but here he was, like me, walking alone along a deserted Soho street at 10am.

I bade him "Good morning," and added "I really enjoyed your programme last night – very funny." He smiled in acknowledgement and we chatted for a few moments. "I would love your autograph," I remarked, "but unfortunately I have neither pen nor paper on me." He searched his pockets and replied "Do you know, neither have I."

To my surprise he invited me to accompany him to the Columbia Film Studios office. It was a grand building, more like an hotel, and we entered and made our way to the reception desk. The girl was on the telephone and busy writing down some message but David spotted someone sitting at a coffee table while I was up to my knees in soft carpeting! David approached the man who was reading his newspaper and spoke to him very quietly.

He, in turn, smiled and tore a piece of newspaper off and handed it over, together with a pen and David duly signed his autograph. I thanked him sincerely before we shook hands and went on our ways.

What an absolute gentleman he was. And that is why, in pride of place and carefully stuck into my autograph book, is his signature – on a torn off piece of newspaper!

EXACTING PERSONAL RETRIBUTION

One thing I learned was that not every manager stuck to the basic rules laid down by the company. I used to attend managers' meetings which were really just pep talks to encourage us to take a fresh look at our stores and try to produce better results. I picked up the best tips, though, from fellow managers at either coffee breaks or lunch. One of the topics was the necessity to be vigilant and keep an eye open for shoplifters, a growing problem at the time. The manager sitting next to me seemed rather disinterested in the speaker's warnings and insistence that all managers follow strict company protocol in case of future reper- cussions. In the coffee break I mentioned to him that he looked bored. "Well," he drawled, "they can say what they like but I have my own method of dealing with people who pinch our stock – they can get us the sack, you know, if you don't spot them and, more importantly, get the word spread around that it is unwise to do it in my own supermarket."

I said, "I share your feelings, and when you have to deal with the police it takes such a lot of time, which we can't really afford, and the fines they receive are never enough.

You hope the publicity will deter others but I'm not so sure. What is your special method of dealing with a shoplifter?" "Well," he drawled again, "When we catch one I take them up to my office and speak to them with no witnesses. I put what they tried to pinch on my desk and say "This is the stuff you tried to take without paying for. Well you can put it back in your bag. You obviously wanted it so you can have it! If I call the police – I take it you don't want me to do that – you will be charged and have a criminal record – which you deserve. For all I know you could have pinched from me before." At this point I help put the stuff in his or her shopping bag, and say, "I reckon that comes to ..." and give a figure way too much and round it up. Then I say "Put the money on my desk for your shopping and get on your way. Don't come back here again and tell any of your mates not to either. OK?" They always pay up – usually with a grim expression but this way I get extra to cover any other shoplifting going on and I think the word goes around – "Don't go there!

I smiled and said, "You're quite a man to have the courage to do that!" "Well," he drawled. "you did ask why I wasn't really listening to all this guff, didn't you?"

IT COULDN'T HAPPEN ... BUT IT DID!

At the end of the day it was entirely my own fault and I certainly learned a lesson from my mistake! There was a wish expressed by everyone in the supermarket to have a sweepstake on the Grand National. On each square of paper was printed a horse running the nation's big race. The paper was duly folded so no one could see the horse's name and all the pieces placed in a small deep box. All those who wanted a horse could then pop his or her hand into the box and pull out their, hopefully, lucky selection!

It so happened that the most garrulous female member of staff I ever had, picked out the slip that said *Foinavon*. The rank outsider with the bookies was at 200-1, then 100-1 at the start of the race. It really had, on form, not the slightest chance of winning and the jockey, John Buckingham, (the guy who normally helped prepare the jockeys behind the scenes) had landed the ride. This member of staff kept telling everyone about how she was going to have the winner and, for once, I made the mistake of reminding her of its betting price. Also, about how it probably shouldn't even have been accepted as a runner.

There were a couple of radios in the store so the staff would know the result when the race had been run. All seemed to be going to plan until a riderless loose horse ran parallel to the 23rd fence, something that caused complete mayhem, with every horse affected. The jockeys either crashed into the fence, had to dismount, or simply stop because of the melee of horses in front of them. *Foinavon* was right at the back of the field but picked its way gently past all the fallen horses and jockeys and continued unhindered, jumping all the fences ahead of it before strolling past the winning post, the winner against all odds of the most prodigious race of all, the Grand National. This loud talkative lady regaled one and all about how she knew it was going to win! She was so excited she couldn't stop talking and I confess I had to take refuge in my office with the door firmly closed. I'm not a bad loser but hearing non-stop how someone picked the 100-1 winner in the National was too much!

A RUDE AWAKENING?

A manager of a nearby supermarket had an ignominious end to his career. It seems the pressure became too much and he began to secretly imbibe around midday at a nearby pub. He'd broken the rules by drinking at all during working hours but one pint became two and even three before he returned on duty. By mid-afternoon there were occasions when he went to a corner of the upstairs warehouse with his order book, around 3.30 in the afternoon "to do the order" he used to say but in truth it was to have a nap. In front of him was an area of flattened cardboard boxes which were temporarily stacked, very handy since he was then out of the way but it was a practice that could only lead to disaster. The staff could see this and deserved better.

One day the stack of cardboard was higher than usual and had become unstable and moved. Whether with the help of a mischievous staff member I'm not sure but it was perilously close to the sleeping manager and had slid virtually on top of him. Not that he knew or cared because he was fast asleep.

It coincided with a director making a surprise visit who enquired where he could find the manager. The staff member was only too willing to point out the comatose man, half submerged under cardboard, sound asleep and oblivious to his unenviable position. "Would you please leave me" hissed the director "and keep everyone out of here until you see me downstairs on the sales floor." What was said or transpired no one knows but the manager, who clearly couldn't cope, was later seen being accompanied to the director's car where he was, apparently, driven to head office a few miles away. He never returned and a new manager arrived a couple of hours later, accompanied by the same director who introduced him to the staff with the news that the previous manager had left the company. Rough but quick justice.

RETIREMENT PARTY AND A LEG-PULL

I once told a story at a fellow supermarket manager's retirement party how he dealt with a customer complaint. It was the end of the day when a woman customer called him over to the fresh chicken display in the chilled cabinet. She had just taken the last one which was a smallish bird. "This is very important," she said to him. "I desperately need a chicken bigger than this to cook tonight." Handing the bird over she pointed out there were none on display and asked if he would look outside in the storage fridge to see if there was a larger one. "Please!" My friend knew there weren't any but to appease the woman he told her he'd have a good look and with the chicken in his hand he left the sales floor.

In the warehouse he spotted a pump on a staff member's bicycle stored in a corner. He promptly borrowed it and, after grabbing some cling film, he inserted it inside the chicken and pumped away ferociously. He then stuffed the hole where the pump had been with a ball of cling film, changed the price label and returned with the new plumper chicken! "Will this do you?" "Oh yes!" she replied, "That's much better. Thank you very much." Just as my friend was turning away feeling rather smug, the lady suddenly added, "Tell you what. I've just been thinking – I'll take the other one as well!"

The whole company roared with laughter, whilst my friend protested his innocence loud and long.

THE WINE CELLAR

One blessing about seminars and pep talks that supermarket managers had to attend, was the opportunity to enjoy a laugh and swap stories. Some managers were real characters with great tales to tell.

One mature manager told of his time as a youngster in a large and well respected recently converted supermarket. Some of the old shop's features had thankfully been retained, including the giant traditional old wooden serving counter which had been re-sited in front of the spirits, wines and beers shelves. One regular elderly customer, a retired colonel, constantly complained about the selection of wines available. He had been used to personal service all his life and did not approve of the conversion to self service. The manager recognised this and came up with a solution! On the bottom shelf but out of the colonel's vision behind the main counter, he placed a selection of hard to sell, discontinued old wines that had been simply gathering dust. Staff avoided this character at all costs but the wily old manager would greet him most cordially and ask how he could help him that day. The colonel regularly topped up his wine cabinet and asked the manager to recommend some good quality brands. The manager would reply in discreet undertones "I'll just go down to the cellar and have a look at our old wines and see if there's one for you. What is it today, red or white?" This "special customer" would then whisper which kind he would prefer.

It was a complete charade because there was no wine cellar at all and the manager – not unlike the old music hall funny walk artiste, Max Wall – would take three slow steps forward behind the counter and through bending his knees, he was seen to "descend" the stairs to the imaginary cellar. He would remain crouched for a minute or two, meanwhile selecting a couple of dusty bottles from the bottom shelf, before ascending the imaginary cellar stairs.

"I've selected a couple of bottles from the stock of the old shop that I'd put aside, one of which should do you nicely!" "I'll have them both – and thank you my good man, thank you," the colonel would reply. The manager wrapped them up and fixed the charge which the colonel always willingly paid. The staff were sworn to secrecy on the grounds that the old chap had received personal service and always left happy.

He did this for ages and was never found out.

ONE OF THE OLD
CHELSEA PENSIONERS

A heart-warming incident involving a show business star that I'll never forget, occurred when I was managing the company's Catford supermarket. I always tried to present a friendly, approachable face to customers, believing it was in the interests of trade and customer relations. After only a few words with a retired male customer, he asked me where I originally came from. I didn't mind answering his question and told him I was from Aberdeen.

"Oh, I know where that is," he replied. "I played in a couple of theatres there in my time. I was part of a comedy duo called Morris and Cowley." I was temporarily stunned, because, as a theatre lover, I'd gone to see the great George Formby when he came north as part of a show in 1958 at the Majestic Theatre in Aberdeen's Union Street, and also on the bill were … Morris and Cowley! "I saw you," I cried, "… when you were on the George Formby Show – you were also introduced as The Chelsea Pensioners and you wore the old red uniforms. I know it was you – I'm right, aren't I?" His face broke into a huge smile and he happily confirmed I was correct – it had been them I'd seen on stage. "Well, well, well," I added, "it's a small world! Tell me, where else did you play?" I was genuinely curious to know, since, although I had enjoyed their stage act, I knew little else about them. "Tomorrow," he said, "I'll bring in my album for you to see – I'm sure you'll be interested to see it. What time would be best?" "10.30 in the morning," I replied, "and we'll have a cup of tea or coffee, and I'm really looking forward to seeing your album."

Little did I think I was to be treated to the most fascinating insight into the past world of old time music hall and interesting old theatres. In 1926 Dave Morris had worked with his partner, Gene Patton – whom he'd met in Blackpool – at the Bristol Hippodrome. Morris and Cowley were originally comedians and dancers. As a duo they played two old soldiers – The Chelsea Pensioners – and they also did other routines for which they became famous, including The Cricketers, which apparently involved much cavorting about on stage. They even introduced a singing style that was close to rapping – even in those olden days! Gene Patton had a family of four sons, two of whom also took to the stage. From their appearances at the Bristol Hippodrome and elsewhere, Morris and Cowley graced the stages of many theatres from 1926 to 1959 and in their early days shared both bills and theatres with many household names, including Sandy Powell, George Robey, Lesley "Hutch" Hutchinson, Tommy Handley, Dickie Henderson,

Stanley Holloway, Ted Ray and Max Miller. When I saw them in Aberdeen, George Formby was top of the bill but they also worked for a time with Formby's brother, Frank. So many great names, so many famous venues. As a theatre buff, I felt transported back in time to another era.

Just before he left, I presented him with a small hamper of fruit, which he was delighted to receive. As we stood at the bottom of the aisle outside my office I whispered to him, "When you left the stage looking like a couple of old and weary soldiers, you suddenly leapt in the air and clicked your heels together to show there was actually plenty of life in you still left. It had made me laugh back then. Could you do that now – just to remind me – when there's nobody about? Can you do it in this aisle?" And so he did. Hearing me chuckle, he glanced over his shoulder, and then made his way to the end of the aisle but not before doing the little routine for a last time. He looked round and smiled, only this time there was an audience standing next to me, of six shoppers, who I'd held back pointing ahead to Dave Morris. We all spontaneously clapped in appreciation. In return, he made two quick professional bows and left the store, smiling. Shortly after our meeting I was transferred to another supermarket and sadly never saw him again but the memory of these two meetings will remain with me forever.

SMILE BUT SAY NO!

That morning, on my way to the company's bank it occurred to me that since I'd be meeting the manager by appointment, he'd be the man to give me some advice. I walked up to the till and announced to the chap behind the counter "I'm Mr. MacLeod, the new manager of the supermarket in Golders Green just down the road." He grinned – a sardonic one, with a definite hint of amusement.

He turned to his left and then to his right and announced to all the tellers "This is the next, sorry new, manager of the Golders Green supermarket." He lowered his voice, but said in what was an audible whisper, "Yes folks, yet another one!" I heard a titter of laughter and was certainly not amused. I took my position seriously and wasn't going to stand for this kind of treatment. I beckoned with my hand for the fresh-faced lad to lean forward across the counter towards the glass front, at the same time leaning forward myself until there was just a small gap between our respective faces. I put the index finger of my left hand to my lips to indicate I wanted quiet, and then said in a loud clear voice that they'd all hear, "At least none of you lot could even think about managing that store, and if you are all so smart, why are you simply serving the public in a bank behind a counter? Now, get me your branch manager and tell him I want to speak to him, and I'll wait until he's available, because I certainly now want a few words with him!" I did this for devilment and my own self-respect, and to let the conceited bank employees know I wasn't to be messed about with, even if I was the 21st manager in seven years to report to the bank!

There was a stunned silence. Nobody knew what to say. The lad simply nodded and went off to find the manager. He came back to see me, I have to confess, more quickly than I'd thought he would, and ushered me into a small office where after a short meeting he wished me "The very best of luck." "I wonder," I asked him, "….. if you could possibly give me some advice about managing in this area? As you will know, the store has been the early career death-knell of too many before me so, as a manager yourself, what words of advice could you give me? I'll be most grateful."

He studied me for a few seconds and then looked me straight in the eye. "You'll find your customers will approach you always looking for a deal, price reduction or concession. Smile but always say 'no'". With that he smiled, wished me luck again, shook my hand, and left, I'll swear with a smile on his face. He clearly knew what I didn't but he also knew I'd soon find out.

Golders Green was like no other supermarket I'd managed before or since, and was a real managerial baptism of fire. On my third morning at approximately 9.30am, I was hailed on the shop floor by a sophisticated, dapper well-dressed man in his early-fifties. "Good morning Mr MacLeod," was his greeting. I pinched myself. Was I that well known here already? Well, I was the manager, after all. "Mr MacLeod," he continued, "You won't of course know this yet but I am a regular customer here and realise as the new manager you will not know me yet. Well, I just couldn't believe what I've gone and done. I live just down the road from here and I've just gone round the store and done my usual shopping." At this point he turned and, with outstretched hand, pointed to his trolley laden with various food items. "Well I was on my way to the till when I realised I'd left both my money, wallet and cheque book at home in my other jacket, having forgotten to transfer them to the one I'm wearing. Can you believe that? I really must be getting old. Well, thing is I don't want to just leave this and walk out of the store because, after I get home I have to dash to an appointment and won't be able to come back until the early afternoon. Now, if the girl on the till, with your permission, could ring this up and keep the receipt in the till until I get back in the afternoon, that would be dandy. Look, I'm hardly likely to disappear and I do assure you most solemnly that I'll return with the money. Please, Mr MacLeod, can you do this as a big favour on this one occasion?"

"Sorry, sir," I replied, "but the company rules state quite clearly that we do not give credit under any circumstances whatsoever. I've been with this company for years and I do know that, and I'm sorry but I can't help you – much as I'd like to, but there it is." He was not, however, ready to accept my refusal and upped the charm offensive. "Oh, Mr MacLeod, I do see your standpoint and respect that but having spent time in your store doing all this shopping, I don't want to have to come back later and do it again. Even if you kept this intact – there's items that have to go into the refrigerator and freezer – all a nuisance. Oh please, Mr MacLeod, I'm sure you can use your position, your authority, to sanction this – just this once, I do assure you!" He smiled what I judged to be a genuine smile and raised his eyebrows in a pleasing manner.

"I'll tell you what I'll do," I said resignedly. "We'll ring through all your shopping and I'll personally put a cheque in the till to cover it until you return with the money which we'll put in the till and I'll remove the cheque from it. Just this once mind. I'll do this for you. It's something I've never done before, so don't let me down." "What!" he replied, looking slightly offended. "No chance, no chance!" I got the cashier to ring up his shopping, which I paid for by cheque. The cashier looked at me rather quizzically but did as she was requested.

By 2pm there was no sign of the gentleman, nor was there by 4pm or indeed by closing time. I already felt more than a little apprehensive, but thought I'd accept defeat by the end of day two, which I did. I never saw him again.

The words of the bank manager haunted me … "Say 'no' and always say 'no'!" I was plagued for a spell, as all previous managers had been, by customers asking for deals such as "If I buy a dozen, what discount will you give me? or "What's the case rate?" etc.

Smile and say 'no'. Words I would never forget.

THE GREAT ESCAPE

It was a bright, dry morning as I walked along the pavement to my store to start my second day as the new manager. From some 40 yards away, I saw the bakery van pull in at the kerbside opposite the recessed glass-fronted entrance doors. The delivery driver quickly pulled trays of bread stacked high from the back of the van onto the pavement before closing the van doors and locking them. Even if he'd looked my way he'd not have recognised me and he'd not have expected to see the manager walk any distance to the store since most had cars. I smiled as he pushed the three stacks of trays of bread into the recessed entrance, knowing full well he was still going to have to wait till I opened up, and I wasn't going to break into a trot to get there, not for a delivery man and with a hard day ahead. I couldn't, however, understand why the baker had not returned to the pavement where he'd have normally stood looking for the manager to arrive and open up. If it had been raining, he'd have returned to his cab. I glanced at my watch which showed it was not yet 7am so I was not late.

A nightmare thought then struck me. If he was actually inside it meant – horror upon horror – that I had not locked the doors the night before. By now I had almost reached the windows where I could see the back of the tills and the ends of the fitments, including the bakery shelves. Hardly daring to breathe, I peered in and saw the delivery-man kneeling down filling the bottom shelves with white sliced loaves. The three stacks of bread were also in front of the shelves. Oh no! I had left the doors unlocked from 6pm until 7am. Fortunately, I kept a cool head and, after checking the baker had his back to the window, slipped past quickly and reached the entrance doors. I opened one silently and, equally silently, with a pounding heart, tiptoed down the main aisle until I reached the stairs at the side that led upstairs to the warehouse and manager's office. Now, halfway up the stairs, I stopped, turned and then clattered my way down as noisily as I could, pausing at the foot to switch on all the lights.

Before I even saw the delivery, I yelled, "Morning Mr Baker!" and approached him with a friendly grin. He was startled but recovered quickly and said, "Do you know, when I came in the front door this morning with the bread as I always do, I could have sworn there was nobody in the store. I thought it can't be but you know – for a second that's what I thought." "Ah!" I replied, "I don't blame you one little bit for that. I had to dash upstairs for a minute and thought I heard your van draw up – you know how quiet it is at this time – and looked out of my office window where I saw you take the three lots of bread out of the back of your van – the trays with the buns and pastry goods last. Where I come from you could trust the baker (which was a lie) because you saw him same time each morning, so I didn't dash down the stairs immediately. I take it I can trust you O.K. – looks like you're doing a good job displaying the bread, tidy and straight. Well done. Have you got the invoice? May I please have a look to see what our bread sales are like?"

Now recovered, relaxed and pleased to have received an unexpected compliment, the baker was as courteous and respectful as could be. I chatted to him amiably until he'd finished his delivery, signed his invoice and was ready to go. "Well, nice to meet you. Sorry to have startled you. Just wanted to see how you were with nobody looking over your shoulder! That display's fine. Thanks, ta ta."

As he drove off I breathed a sigh of relief. I'd got away with disaster, not once but twice. If someone had sheltered in the recessed entrance and leaned against the entrance doors after closure, they'd have swung open and created the perfect opportunity for anyone to rob the store at will. What headline would that have made in the London press, indeed the national press? And …. if the baker had realised beyond argument that I'd left the store open all night, the story would have reached every store in the company and head office that very morning. Happily, neither of these things happened, and I'd been a very lucky boy indeed.

Will I ever learn?

Head office sent me a letter with a cheque attached which had bounced. One of my customers had passed it, and it was signed "Mrs K L Sherwood [not her real name]. I asked the cashiers if the name rang a bell and one said it did and the woman had shown proof that she worked at the American Embassy and was adamant her credentials were genuine. I told them not to let her through again without calling me, which they did when she reappeared. She'd filled her trolley and had reached the till. I was called, and asked her to come to my office. She was extremely convincing and showed me up-to-date references from the American Embassy and explained that her money was late in arriving from the USA, where she'd previously lived, and that it was simply a technical hitch that would be resolved quickly. Convinced, I allowed her to pay by cheque, and told the cashier to ring the shopping through.

I hadn't calculated on her smartness. She returned again that afternoon and bought some more shopping – and went to the same till telling the cashier that I'd okayed her cheque. This having been done in the morning, the cashier believed her. And so, I ended up by being told off by head office, that there were now three cheques bouncing, and it appeared that, if they were presented again, they'd be rejected.

I went to her Golders Green address but got no answer. I contacted the American Embassy, and remember the person at the end of the line there sighing heavily and saying, "She is no longer with us, and we'd say the same to you as we have to just about every other trader in Golders Green. She appears to be bankrupt and, frankly, you've no chance of getting your money back. Sorry." And they were right. Would I ever learn? I began to seriously wonder, yet the supermarket was doing well, trade was up, standards were fine, head office was pleased.

It was a bank holiday when my first managerial fallout happened. I'd been working like a dog and our trade had been phenomenal. Late afternoon a director from head office arrived. Sure the floor could do with a brush and some of the shelves were becoming depleted with queues on each till. When I got the call to the checkout I was up to my eyes helping out in the warehouse. Who the heck wanted me? Without so much as an introduction, though I knew who he was, I was asked aggressively, "Why have you not put up all the coloured posters sent to you of the fresh foods special offers? Do you know how much they cost?"

He was talking, would you believe, about bacon offers, ham offers, and pork chops offers. I had remembered where the supermarket was situated and decided they were inappropriate. I attempted to explain but not used to being questioned, he ranted at me, "We are a corporate company and you will do exactly as directed, do you understand?" I attempted again to explain why this was not the right policy in respect of the store's situation in the high street. "Mr MacLeod," he fumed, "You just won't listen will you? You don't understand, it seems, that you must always adhere to company policy. This is because you're either too obstinate or perhaps it's because you're Scottish." He turned on his heel and left, vigorously shaking his head. I said something under my breath and resumed my store duties. At the end of the day I knew we'd done extremely well – how well I didn't know but was about to find out.

Late on Tuesday morning after the holiday, the telephone rang. It was the company's managing director. "Hello Mr. MacLeod," said the voice, and I knew who it was. "How are you today?" In my usual forthright manner, I replied that I was well but not particularly happy. He replied saying, "I believe you had a visit from Mr. March over the holiday period."

And before he could continue, I interjected, "Yes. He came when we were all up to our eyes and doing our best to cope and keep all the customers happy. Yes, I was in a rather dirty overall, and yes the store could have looked better, but trade was tremendous. It really was." "Mr MacLeod," interjected the managing director, in a strong voice. I realised my suppressed anger had been detected and I was about to be told off. "I'm phoning to congratulate you. The store's takings have never been higher and the weekend trade was an all time record. Pass on my congratulations to your staff, and my personal thanks for their efforts. I shall be sending you a letter to put up on your staff notice board. Now then, Mr. MacLeod, I do believe you had a bit of an altercation with Mr. March over advertising, and that you got a bit hot under the collar. Well now, I want you to put all that behind you. Don't worry about it, forget it, and just you carry on there like you're doing. Well done, again."

"Thank you," I replied, completely humbled. "Thank you very much." Clearly the managing director saw where I was coming from and was a fair man. Calls like that lifted you and added to your confidence.

ROBBERY WITH VIOLENCE

Without warning the office door was kicked open. It was 8pm on a Friday in Catford and, lying on my desktop in my office in the store, were the takings for the busiest day of the week. Some of it was in leather bank wallets and the rest lay in neat banded stacks alongside. "Let's have the effing money – NOW," yelled this figure in white overalls. For a split second I thought it might just be some incredibly stupid joke, until I spotted the large ornate wooden shillelagh he was wielding above his head. "Give us the effing money!" he continued to bellow.

My immediate reaction was then to prevent him getting to the money and, impulsively, I resisted. He tried to bring the club down on my head but, due to the sloping ceiling of the small office, the head of it smashed through the plasterwork and lodged temporarily in the mesh wire behind. Extracting it quickly, he then swung it wildly, finally catching me on the shoulder.

The impact spun me around and I then received a knee in the back from a second person who now joined in, and I was viciously kicked and bundled to the floor. My assistant manager then landed with a thud on the floor to my left, and I could see that his hands were tied to his back. The poor fellow had been just about to lock the store door, following the departure of the last staff member, when he was grabbed by someone attired in shop overalls and promptly frog-marched quickly and quietly to the office.

My ankles were tied to my wrists and, as I lay there trussed up, my mind was amazingly calm. I realised that, after it was all over, the police would ask for any information that could assist them. I turned my head around at the precise moment that my female clerk was being tied up. She was sitting on her chair and also appeared remarkably calm in the circumstances. Suddenly the scarf, which was tied around the thug's face, fell below his chin, and I saw his face quite clearly.

"Pull your scarf up!" shouted the villain standing above me. "He could have seen you!" There was a sudden silence. "Look," said the same voice, "If he moves again, just blow his effing head off." A figure knelt on the floor beside my head, there was the loud click of a gun being cocked and the end of the barrel of a sawn-off shotgun was placed on my temple. I was sweating so much that the perspiration was blocking my nostrils and with my face pressed hard against the tiled floor, my breathing was becoming nearly impossible. It was at this moment I thought I was going to die – by asphyxiation or worse by drowning on my office floor! I moved my head slightly to get breath – I had to. He obviously and thankfully didn't pull the trigger.

The telephone wires were ripped out and the removal of money began.

The safe was emptied and the wallets gathered together. Suddenly, the sound of a police car siren was heard outside. "Can't be them," snapped one of them, "No reason." Sadly, the sound of the klaxon horn died away as the patrol car sped past the store, the occupants totally oblivious of what was going on under their noses. Meanwhile, the manager of the nearby Bromley supermarket was innocently passing by, saw the store lights on and rattled the door intending to speak to me. One of the gang in white overalls opened the door, yanked him inside where he too was tied up and left on the floor.

"Right," said the one in charge. "If any of you move before we're gone, you'll get it – so stay put." With that they were gone. There was no way they'd be looking back I concluded so somehow I hoisted myself up from the floor and, remembering there was a Stanley knife in my desk, managed to open the drawer. Without any difficulty, I found the knife and immediately attempted to cut the clerk free. It was tricky, and unfortunately the knife blade touched her tights. "Sorry," I exclaimed, "I've made a hole in your tights I'm afraid!" "Never mind that," said the clerk with a hint of laughter in her voice, "Just cut me free, please!" This done, she, in turn, cut me free, after which we both ventured out of the office. "Don't forget me," cried a voice from the office! "Oh, dear! Sorry!" I replied, and I asked my clerk to do the necessary and cut the others free as well, whilst I rushed out to the street and found someone who thankfully contacted the local police station.

The police arrived within minutes and the three of us now stood together. "How are you?" my clerk asked me, "Didn't you realise, when you looked up from the floor, the other bloke was watching you – and kicking you?" I had been totally unaware of this but my back was certainly now aching like mad. "How are you?" I asked my assistant manager, "You look really white." "Only me and my washing machine will ever know how scared I have been," he replied quietly. Pointing to my female clerk, I addressed the detectives. "She was so calm throughout, and so brave – for a woman." "Never mind woman," said one of the detectives. "I reckon she was brave for a man!"

The detectives then took statements from the three of us, whilst the fingerprinting experts dusted the office. While this was taking place our area manager, who had been contacted by the police on our behalf, arrived. During the previous visits I'd noted that he had a tendency towards making sarcastic remarks, something I detested. This was not the time for any comments but he was true to form. His opening line was, "Okay – how much did they get away with?" This, before he knew anything about the night's events! My clerk, normally a most reserved individual, saw red. "Is that all you can say?" she yelled at him. "Is that all you can say after what we've been through – how much money gone – not how are you or are you hurt? You disgust me." She spat the last few words out and flounced off to the toilet. "I didn't mean ..." he burbled, but by now each of us had turned our backs on him and checked that our statements were sufficient for the CID.

It suddenly hit me that by now my wife would have expected me home more than two hours ago and I had not been able to telephone to explain my lateness. The CID would be back the following morning for more details, but we were now thankfully, free to go home. "Where on earth have you been?" asked my wife on my return. "Why didn't you phone if you were going to be so late? I thought something terrible must have happened to you, I was so worried." Explaining, in as low a key as I could, what had happened, was not easy. Needless to say she was shocked, upset, and finally relieved that I was home. My back and ribs were badly bruised and painful but it didn't seem to matter. It was time for bed and I had to open up at 6.30am next day regardless of anything – which I did. The others also turned up at their usual time. No such thing as counselling in those days!

In the days that followed, detectives investigating the robbery were pleased with the information I was able to give them – accents, conversation, a Christian name but best of all a racial description. I was taken to Scotland Yard and shown large posters of known criminals and was able to identify the thug in question straight away. Within a week they'd made an arrest, but warned me that they would not be pulling in the other two villains, although they knew who they were, since they were already under surveillance for bigger crimes, and that the CID were playing a waiting game. "You'll get police protection," said the detective, "and you'll have to go to court as witness when the time comes. OK?" What exactly "police protection" was I never found out!

From the dock of the Old Bailey, I looked ahead at a face I had seen once before. If looks could kill I'd have been dead, as I nearly was before. Looking around the court-room I could see representatives of the company I worked for amongst a sea of deadly-serious faces and, of course gentlemen in grey wigs that looked like they belonged to a different age.

"On the night of Friday, 15th November, 1967, around 8pm, after you had brought all the monies from the tills of your store into the office, did anything unusual or untoward happen?" asked a fellow in a grey wig, raising his eyes questioningly in my direction. The judge, I observed, was now leaning forward in my direction. I pondered my reply, while looking at the accused who'd seen me getting kicked black and blue, and nearly getting my head blasted off. Totally unused to Old Bailey court language, and being young at the time – to me using the word unusual was taking the mick!

At this critical moment you could have heard a pin drop. I decided to bide my time and simply answered, "Yes." "Would you," asked the fellow in the grey wig, for a second time, "like to tell the Court what unusual occurrence took place?" I was once again conscious of the crowded court-room and the rows of unblinking eyes which appeared to be staring intently at me. At times like this some people do daft things, and I'm afraid I'm one of them. "Well" I answered, deliberately slowly … "Just for once, the cash taken from all the tills, balanced first time!"

At this the courtroom erupted into gales of laughter and, now realising what I'd done, I wondered if I'd be reprimanded or worse – charged with contempt of court! "Was there anything else?" asked the judge. He was close enough for me to see a twinkle in his eye, much to my relief. I gave my evidence clearly and in full and the case proceeded smoothly. The accused was found guilty of armed assault and playing his part in the £2,000 plus robbery, a tidy sum which would at the time have purchased a three bedroom house in London. To the utter disgust of many, however, he was given a sentence of only two years in prison.

After the Old Bailey court case, Scotland Yard police officers took me out to lunch. The officers explained that they knew two other members of the gang but since they were involved in other crimes and under surveillance, they did not want to bring them yet. They said the two year sentence was no deterrent whatsoever to crimes of this nature and that, sadly, nothing would change after he got out. How right they were!

On Friday, 7th March, 1972 my assailant at Catford was part of a group, led by a notorious gangster, who were involved in a bungled robbery of a jewellers in Blackpool. The police, however, had received a tip off that the crime was to take place and were keeping the shop under surveillance. The jeweller was badly beaten up and the shop ransacked before the thugs fled. In the chase that followed, Sewell (my second assailant) shot Police Superintendent Gerry Richardson dead. Another chasing policeman, Sergeant Ian Hampson, was also shot and seriously injured.

All the gang were eventually captured, including my assailant who I had given witness against at the Old Bailey following the gang's raid on my supermarket. He was sentenced to 25 years for the attempted murder of Sergeant Ian Hampson, 20 years for manslaughter of Superintendent Richardson, 15 years for conspiracy and 15 years for armed robbery. The gang leader, who killed Superintendent Richardson, received concurrent sentences totalling 80 years.

When I read this in the *Daily Mirror* a distinct chill swept over me. I now fully realised the lengths that this gang were prepared to go to, to escape being caught and brought to justice. With this in mind, I realised that my own life must, indeed, have hung by a thread at the time of the robbery at my store. When I now reflect on the full and interesting life that I've been privileged to live and enjoy, I find it difficult to accept that capital punishment is not the appropriate sentence for those who murder innocent people who are simply doing their job – as the Law puts it, for "pecuniary advantage". Only those who have been close to death in circumstances like mine and have survived, can truly understand how it feels when they read about someone else who too had faced a loaded gun but who had not been so lucky.

CHARMED LIFE

Over-confidence or complacency is something that most managers will admit to experiencing at some time in their careers, and I'm one who was guilty, particularly on one occasion that could have resulted in serious consequences. It was a clear company ruling that, when money wallets were dropped into the night safes, the manager was always accompanied by another male member of staff, for obvious security reasons. You could hardly believe that I chose to ignore this ruling whilst manager of a supermarket in London's Soho! Sadly it's true.

It was almost 5.30 p.m. and the three wallets filled with notes were ready to be dropped into the night safe some half a mile from the supermarket. Everybody was busy wrapping things up in their departments as closing time approached and, although I should have chosen somebody to accompany me, I thought I'd be safe enough and that it would save reducing the number of staff on the shop floor. I told the office clerk I was going on my own and would not listen to the warning that I really shouldn't. "I'll be fine," I assured her and pushing the wallets inside my jacket, I left the store. Irresponsible? Yes, most certainly, especially since I began to quickly wonder if the bulkiness of my jacket was a giveaway. I kept my eyes wide open and the chute in the wall of the bank that I could now see, was a welcome sight. The bank was situated on the corner of a crossroads and, thankfully, I was almost there. The wallets were still concealed when I glanced across the road and saw two men first look at each other, then nod and make their way instantly across the road towards me. Incredibly there was no other person around. Their intentions were very clear and I realised I was in trouble, and, without a second's delay, I fled. Fortunately, I was very fit, raced across the road and flew down the street opposite. Looking behind I realised the two pursuers were not in sight and I opened the heavy wooden door of a building and closed it quickly. I was now faced with a stairway that led to the building's first floor, and raced to the top of it, and opened the first door I saw and entered. Now facing me were at least two dozen men who were busy sewing leather bags and the like. One stood up, and, with a frown, asked me what I wanted. I simply could not contemplate telling him the truth, since I did not know them nor could I obviously trust them. I asked if a fictitiously-named man worked there, claiming I had been told he did and that I needed to speak to him. He replied in broken English that he did not. I apologised for disturbing them and quickly left, and made my way down the stairs. I opened the door just far enough to see some distance down the street.

Fate was on my side. They were still there, scanning the street, thankfully with their backs to me. I closed the door immediately and silently climbed the stairs, keeping out of sight of the door. I waited there for what seemed an eternity and then made my way down to the door once again. With heart in mouth I opened it slightly and there was no one now in sight. I waited until I was sure I could make the dash to the bank, which I did. Glancing round the corner there was still no sign of them, and I quickly dropped the wallets down the chute to safety.

To say I was relieved would be an understatement. It was at that moment I realised that they would by now be alarmed back at my store, so ran as quickly as I could until, breathless, I reached it. The clerk had, in fact by now telephoned the police and informed them regarding my absence, assuming something bad must have happened. It was after all Soho in the 1960s. As quickly as I could I telephoned the police and assured them I was safe and had merely met someone who'd delayed me, and apologised if this had caused a problem.

I confided in the clerk what had actually happened, and she shook her head and said I should have listened to her and that muggings and street robberies were not uncommon. She asked me if I was aware of this. I had to confess I was not, and it was only my fitness that had prevented me being not only a victim but resultantly seriously breaking the rules, and probably receiving a company warning. My guardian angel had clearly been working overtime. I'd also learned an important lesson, and used my experience and this story in future years to deter other managers from taking short cuts when it came to security – particularly if it involved cash. Lucky? I'll say I was!

DOING MY BIT TO HALT
A NASTY CRIME

In South London I was involved with the same "nick" which was situated just across the road in Camberwell, quite frequently. They were getting to know me quite well due to the many incidents that, sadly, became part of my life each week. I remember one incident very well and it always gives me a smile. The adjacent area at Brixton, was plagued incessantly by a particularly nasty form of thieving. Customers, usually housewives, had a bad habit of leaving their purses far too readily available for opportunistic theft, and a threesome were exploiting this to the full, with a tried and tested formula.

On checkout queues, the female member of the trio would deftly remove the purse from the shopping bag of a waiting shopper and immediately pass it under cover to the chap standing alongside her in the queue. He, in turn, slipped it to the third chap, who promptly disappeared from the location altogether. When the shopper discovered her purse had gone seconds after she'd last seen it, she'd accuse the couple behind her – who pleaded innocence. "Search us, search us!" The police were aware of the method used but he had no luck in solving this heartless mode of theft. One day it was especially busy around midday, when I heard a lady's scream coming from the checkout area. I was working in the main aisle at the time and immediately dashed towards the tills. At that precise moment, a smallish fellow in a blue checked shirt and navy jeans, raced past me and out through the entrance door and into the street. Should I chase him or go to the till? I chose the latter, and found an hysterical mum with a small child, crying "I know you've taken it – it was there when I was standing here", and she then burst into tears. "We didn't take it, we didn't take it," protested the couple behind her. I had to do something quickly, so I ushered the remaining queue to the adjacent tills and told the three involved, plus the cashier, to stay put while we got the police. The couple appeared hurt, yet relaxed, about the accusations. The woman whose purse had been stolen, on the other hand, remained distraught.

I told the police officer very quickly that I'd noticed this fellow run out of the store and up the hill, and described him. One of the two officers present immediately left and drove off up the hill in pursuit. The trio and the policeman made their way to my office. A policewoman who I fortunately knew arrived quickly. "We've organised an identity parade," she told me quietly, "and we need your help." "We have caught and apprehended someone running up the hill and simply want you to identify him. Okay?" "But,"

I replied quickly, "All I saw was the back of his head, his height and what he was wearing. I would really love to help you because I know the misery that's been caused but I didn't see quite enough of the guy who ran away. I'm just not certain I can guarantee I'll be able to point him out." "Of course you'll be able to do it, don't worry, you will!" And we then walked to the door of the room where inside a number of men were duly lined up and waiting.

A policeman opened the door quietly about an inch wide, beckoned to me and whispered, "He's the last one on the right." With that, he opened the door fully and prodded me into the room. I walked along the line, looking at each man in turn, until I came to the end of the line, where I made my identification. I was then led out. "Are you sure?", I asked the officer. "You are sure, aren't you?" "Of course," he replied. "Positive. You'll find this will stop what has been going on, thank heavens. Right – you may return to your store, Mr. MacLeod!", he added with a beaming smile.

Thankfully for my conscience, what he assured me was exactly what happened and three guilty pleas and convictions followed. My conscience was clear. My action helped to stop any further instances of this nasty local crime. Yet, I was occasionally plagued by the thought, what if .....?

A QUIET HERO AND A GREAT FRIEND

John Bower only just survived D-Day. A quiet hero and dear friend of mine for more than 45 years, he was manager of a supermarket in Marlborough, Wiltshire, for over 35 years. We were both members and prize-winners of The Institute of Certificated Grocers and sometimes worked together in the trade.

In France, John's tank unit was involved in a street battle in the Normandy town of Lisieux, where all the tanks of the 1st Northamptonshire Yeomanry were destroyed. John and his driver managed to get out of theirs, as flames engulfed it, only to be met by gunfire from the waiting Germans. They ran down the street but were both hit, yet they found cover and managed to return to their regiment. They were sent back to England, where they were treated for their wounds before being transferred back to Normandy.

In the area near St. Lo, they again encountered German tanks. John's was positioned parallel to the road and was unspotted by the enemy. They remained motionless until the Germans were almost upon them – then they opened fire and destroyed all four enemy tanks. In one was SS

Commander and German tank legend, Michael Wittmann, who had been responsible for destroying 138 British tanks. The regiment was credited with this outstanding achievement and went on to relieve the village of St. Aignan. John has since returned there many times to a wonderful official reception.

Each year he personally prints the names of all those in the 1st and 2nd Northamptonshire Yeomanry who gave their lives, 87 and 89 soldiers respectively, onto wooden crosses with, and the resulting wreath is taken to Whitehall by his son, Brian. Every year too, John can be seen with his poppy tray in Marlborough Town Square – he must surely be one of the oldest poppy sellers in the country!

Relatively recently he was retrospectively awarded France's highest military medal, the Legion d'Honneur which was formally presented to him in 2016. He was also invited to the VE Celebration for veterans at Horse Guards Parade Ground in Whitehall, where he was introduced to Prince Charles and the Duchess of Cornwall, and the then Prime Minister, David Cameron.

A REAL TEST OF MY METTLE

I'd been called to the rear door of the warehouse – it had sounded like an emergency – and it was. A few yards from the door we had a shed where we kept all our cardboard which had to be tied up in parcels or bales for collection. Looking out from the shed's entrance was the young lad who'd been tying some up. Immediately in front of him, staring at him from a distance of about three yards, was an enormous rat.

Transfixed, they neither moved nor, it seemed, even blinked at each other. By now a silent group of staff stood next to me, wondering what was going to happen. I removed the flat wrought-iron bar that was used to add security to the large wooden nearby doors and, with my heart in my mouth, silently and slowly moved up behind the rat. I raised the bar above my head, holding it with two hands and with total concentration and power, brought it crashing down on this huge rodent.

When I opened my eyes (having closed them at the moment of impact) the rat was now about three feet in the air, falling with a thud on the tarmac. I was shaking, but aware of my position as manager, simply told the lad to come forward and that he was quite safe, and then turned and walked to the back doorway. The watching staff all burst into instant applause and "Well dones" filled the air!

I asked one of them to get the rat put into the outside large dustbin, replaced the iron bar and then whispered, "Could someone bring a cup of tea to my office – soon as possible!" Never did a cup of tea requested take less time to arrive, and equally never was it more welcome!

None of the staff would ever know how nervous I was as I killed that rat – but take it from me – I was! I got the rodent extermination company to come the same day and they went into the foundations of the store where they shot a number of them and also left enough poison to, thankfully, have the desired effect.

NOT AT ALL HOW IT APPEARED!

A friend of mine from North of the Border, visited me at my supermarket at Berwick Street in Soho. I was happy to see him because at that moment I had to make a visit to the bank in Wardour Street. He accepted my invitation to accompany me. It was a walk I made daily and around 10 am I'd greet and be greeted by most of the night club owners who were outside supervising the cleaning of the front of their respective clubs.

After I'd spoken to the fourth proprietor, my pal stopped walking suddenly, looked at me in amazement and remarked "Do you visit all these clubs? Goodness me!" I explained the strictly business relationship I enjoyed with them and he was, on my behalf, clearly relieved!

A GLASGOW RANGERS SUPPORTER

As I entered the supermarket in Kinson, Bournemouth, in order to meet up with three other local managers and a company director, I could not help noticing something was going on at the back of the checkouts. I continued on my way to the small office from which you could see the area quite clearly.

"He's one of his lot", said the director, as I entered the office, "He's the man to deal with it!" The problem was a drunken Scotsman in the till area, attracting the attention of cashiers and customers and who needed ushering out of the store. However, an inebriated man can react to simple requests too often in an unruly and unwanted manner. Hence, as a Scot, I might have the best chance of removing him quietly and without fuss. No pressure on me then!

As I approached, I noted he was wearing a light blue jersey beneath his jacket – which meant to me he was most likely not a Glasgow Celtic fan but a Rangers fan. Pointing at his jersey I took a chance, "Well, well, another Rangers supporter just like myself?" I remarked. His mood was transformed into one of extreme friendliness. Jackpot!

We chatted about the "'Gers" for a few minutes, then I asked him if he'd do me a favour and come back to the store after the director up here (I indicated where he was in the office) had gone. "He's here for an hour and a bit – so if you leave now and come back in two hours, we can have a proper chat – you're a 'Gers man – so put it there", I added, stretching out my hand. He shook it warmly and we made our way to the exit. I then returned to the office in triumph!

When he got the gist of the story the director said, "Good job you were a Rangers supporter." "Actually," I replied, "I'm an Aberdonian – mortal enemy (like Celtic) of Rangers."

I just said and did what I hoped would work – and wasn't I lucky!

A DISASTER CALLED DOUGLAS

With trade picking up and sales increasing in one of my earliest supermarkets in Aberdeenshire, the new boss decided it was time to increase the staffing levels, particularly since he had added managing the delicatessen and dairy counter to my greengrocery responsibilities. In his wisdom, he engaged a 16 year old lad called Douglas whose job brief was simple. In between delivering grocery orders to locals on the bike, he took on some of the more menial tasks, like sweeping up, cleaning, tidying the warehouse etc. and helping on the greengrocery fixture. Normally this would have been a welcome staffing addition but so much depends on the individual.

To say he was slow would be a gross understatement and yet you have to have a secret admiration for people who can somehow string out the length of time it takes to do simple tasks. There must be an art to it and Douglas had the natural talent. I also realised he could be quite cunning. It became noticeable that late on Saturday afternoons, just as the cleaning up, tidying and sweeping had to be commenced, we would receive a telephone call from a customer requesting a delivery of groceries and provisions which, naturally, had to be accepted, processed and delivered by Douglas.

By the time he returned I had, by necessity, completed the weekend cleaning and clearing-up duties, together with all my other responsibilities, in Douglas' absence. After three consecutive weeks I realised this was no coincidence and mentioned it to my landlady at my digs. "Funnily enough" she remarked "that lad delivers the order to the lady across the road – she's his auntie, by the way, he has a late lunch break – according to her – and stays to watch the wrestling on the television."

Mystery solved, I decided to have a quiet word with the boss, since I felt there was a chance that we might actually lose the customer if it was badly handled. "No problem" said the boss with a knowing smile, "when it happens this week I'll personally deliver it by car – you keep the lad's nose to the grindstone in the meantime, O.K.?" It sounded like the perfect solution and it worked splendidly. Douglas was clearly perplexed at the turn of events but clearly felt querying the boss's action might backfire. The late afternoon telephone call on Saturdays quickly ceased.

Whilst I was standing behind the delicatessen on the busiest afternoon of the week, I was suddenly aware of water lapping my shoes and realised we had a leak or burst pipe. Alone with a queue of customers to serve, I caught the boss's attention and he investigated the source immediately but could do nothing about it. The water continued to seep out and reached the sales floor. Customers now aware of it, stared at the floor, but glad to get their requirements, quickly made for the checkout. "The plumber will be here very soon," whispered the boss "keep going until he comes".

By now an ever growing film of water was covering the floor and I started to whisper to him in reply "it could be dangerous" but he had already collared Douglas and ordered him to mop up. With customers still walking around and the water level increasing, the lad managed to do the last thing anybody could have ever wanted to see – somehow tripping over the mop and kicking over the entire bucket of water. As the last customer hurried from the scene, I heard the sickening crash of broken glass, followed by another and another. Dashing, or rather sloshing, my way to the location I was just in time to see a stack of forty plus cardboard cases of bottles of orange, lemon and strawberry squash disintegrate. The water had rendered the base to wet pulp and bottles were crashing from all directions to the floor, multi-coloured streams replacing the clear water. For a few seconds we were all stunned.

"Good grief!!" cried a voice from the shop doorway "whatever is going on?" It was the plumber who had, at last arrived. Ushering him quickly to the area of water leakage the boss whispered tersely "Get the doors shut and for goodness sake organise the cleaning up!" It didn't actually take the plumber many minutes to effect emergency repairs but the cleaning up wasn't so easy – it was months before we felt all areas of the floor were absolutely free from the sticky after-effects!

One particular lunch time I had to fill in as a check-out operator, due to absenteeism. From my position I could see Douglas through an open doorway at the back of the store, which I felt at the time, was some consolation since he definitely needed watching. Because of staffing shortage, he was instructed to weigh and price onions into polythene bags. On the table was a large new scale which he was to use for the purpose but I suddenly realised he was no longer standing by the table. It puzzled me why he'd disappeared but since I was serving a customer, checking up on him would have to wait. Once free, I glanced through the doorway where, to my consternation, one end of the table was slowly rising, whilst the scale was now slowly, and not surprisingly, juddering its way to the table edge. I arrived at the scene at the moment the large scale crashed to the floor ending up smashed to smithereens. Open-mouthed I then witnessed Douglas slowly emerging from under the table.

"What have you done now?" I screamed at him. "Well," he drawled "the table wasn't balanced properly and I went underneath to put a wee bit of wood under the leg, and the next thing I knew was this noise..." "Douglas, just get the bits of the scale in a box, clear up the oil on the floor, and when the boss returns from his lunch you tell him when I'm nowhere near!" Returning to the check-out I served the waiting customer wondering what would be the next catastrophe. As it happened I hadn't long to wait.

The sound of something being broken reached my ears from the preparation area, probably Douglas putting the scale in a box, I thought. Somehow I just wasn't convinced and dashed out once again to find Douglas was crouched under the sink, holding a bottle of disinfectant. "What's happened this time?" I yelled. "Well," he said slowly," I cleaned up the oil but there was a bit of a smell on the table and floor, so I reached up for the bottle of disinfectant on the shelf above the sink and I dropped it." "I see," I replied, "but what was the noise – the bottle's not broken?" "It fell through the sink," he replied, for once, resignedly, "and though the bottle isn't broken, the sink is." "Douglas" I shouted, "when the boss returns from his lunch in a minute and you tell him about the scale and the sink, I don't want to be around."

A minute or two later, Mr. Forbes, the manager returned, and to get to his office he had to pass through the preparation room. I tiptoed to within earshot as he entered. Spotting the fragmented scale in the box he demanded to know how it happened. "It's only a few days old, and now I have to telephone head office for another, what next?" As he numbly reached for the door handle of his office Douglas' plaintive voice again assailed his ears. "By the way, Mr Forbes, there's a hole in the sink." "Yes Douglas," he replied, "that is to let the water run away." "I know that," replied Douglas, "but I'm talking about another hole." A customer queue was beginning to build on the check-out so I never did hear the end of it all but I do know that when I spoke to the boss an hour later there was a distinct smell of whisky on his breath.

Ultimately Douglas received his final warning that any further costly actions would mean the end of his employment. I felt the boss had been remarkably tolerant in the circumstances and recalled Humphrey Bogart once saying "Never give a sucker an even break", and wondered how long Douglas would last. I had only 48 hours to wait for the answer.

A wealthy, local customer ordered a case of his favourite malt whisky and it was Douglas's job to deliver it. He put the case into the basket in the front of the bike and rode off. Sometime later he returned with some bad news. He'd pulled up en-route to speak to someone he knew and forgetting the weight in the basket, he dismounted. It capsized instantly with disastrous consequences with seven bottles flying like projected missiles from the box straight on to the tarmac, each bottle breaking and spilling the contents into the gutter and along the pavement. I feel that for Mr. Forbes, a whisky loving Scot, Douglas had committed the ultimate crime, and really this time he surely had to go.

I learned later that the boss had told him he'd considered suggesting a weekly deduction from his pay packet would help to cover some of the cost of the damage he'd caused but since Douglas was so disaster-prone, this arrangement could well have become permanent and it was therefore in everybody's interest (especially the store's) that his employment was terminated. Whatever became of Douglas I never knew. He was a likeable lad but as a supermarket employee he was a total disaster!

DIDCOT

In the late 1960s I was appointed manager at the company's supermarket in Didcot, Berkshire. I had worked in London for many years previously before requesting a transfer to an available supermarket "in the country." The branch at Didcot was the best they could do. As soon as I arrived I learned the store enjoyed a poor reputation and a succession of poor trading results had necessitated a managerial change.

However, the staff tried hard to please. They worked tirelessly and gradually we turned things around. While all this was happening a member of staff composed this poem about life at the supermarket, and when I re-read it now I have only warm memories about the successful time I enjoyed as manager at good old Didcot.

This was written by Jess. (Sadly I have forgotten her surname. but she was very supportive and to whom I still owe a debt of gratitude – Thanks.)

THE DIDCOT DAILY ROUTINE

Pricerite, Pricerite, is a very large shop
Where staff work like fury, not daring to stop.
Winnie sorts the flowers and Maureen does the cheese.
We smile all the while, trying just to please.
It is a large shop where prices they suit all
The rich the poor, the short and the tall.

Bess is on provisions, young and blonde it's true
But like us is ageing, and now looks fifty-two!
Owen's on the fruit and veg, and poor old Dave too.
Grousing and grumbling, the flipping whole day through.
They pre-pack the spuds, the carrots and greens,
Deserving two crowns these two vegetable queens!
The chappie in charge is a Scot just so high.
He's dashing round like a bluebottle fly.
He works like a dog from morning 'til night
Expressing quite plainly he's losing the fight.
"Don't give up Dear Mac – we're all very true.
We may not be special, but boy what a crew.

We're loyal, we work hard, we do try to please.
Come on now, all smile. Try saying "cheese"!
Jess comes in daily with a sniff and a choke,
Then starts things off with a nice juicy joke.
Most like to listen, but some others will sneer.
A sidelong glance shows they've got a cocked ear.

We've girls on the tills and a lad on the lard,
Boys in the warehouse – they all work quite hard.
Butch cuts the meat, Greg battles with eggs.
No wonder our men have such short hairy legs!
Nina worked here from the start of the shop.
In her two years of slaving she tried not to stop,
But it got her quite bad tired and forlorn
So she upped and away to Australia's Melbourne.

There's others that work here that I've failed to whack.
Betty, Brenda, Joan, Carol and Mac.
And there's dear Vi who does our tea break.
She must surely be sick of teas, rolls and cake!
But her profits and gains keep everything hearty
And her efforts result in our fabulous party.

These words and jokes are just my way
Of describing my shop life day by day.
I enjoy working here – with a smashing staff
'Cos no matter the moans, we have a good laugh!

I wrote this after a work-related journey that took me into lovely Dorset ...

Would you believe it?
Driving along an old Dorset lane
I found myself trailing behind
The most indescribably dirty old van
That you're ever likely to find.

Earth and mud covered roof and sides,
And its windows were black with grime.
To any clean-car conscious person
Its condition was surely a crime.

Yet, there was an understandable reason
Why this van now appeared so obscene,
And there on its filthy old back door
Could the answer be quite clearly seen ...

Daubed through the mud, someone had
printed
In bold letters, the clue that I wanted.
"Please do not wash or clean this vehicle,
.... seedlings planted".

(* Drawn from the book, *Scrumpy and Cream* edited by Dawn Jordan and published in 1992 by Arrival Press.)

117

LANGUAGE THEY UNDERSTOOD

All my working life I was, when it came to using bad language, not guilty. I considered it was unnecessary and often offensive. However, there was a time I threw this personal rule out of the window. It was a rainy early afternoon in Berwick Street, Soho, and the street market traders were sheltering temporarily under my supermarket's overhanging external roof above the long front windows. This would have been just acceptable but a number of them gazed, noses to the window, at the cashiers. To be more precise, at the female cashiers' legs and, in some cases, attractive profiles. They were making very audible and totally inappropriate comments, causing upset to the girls and annoyance to the customers.

This unacceptable situation had to be dealt with, and I was prompted to do it by a lovely mature Italian lady member of staff. It was something the likes of which I'd never had to deal with before. I always trusted my vibes and walked out to confront them very aware that there were passers-by. The traders were not men who I felt would respond to a polite request, and in any case they were not going to get it! I decided to show them up and – without going into detail – did just that. Using language I'd never used before, I publicly and mercilessly belittled them! Cashiers, customers and passers-by all stopped to witness my performance! However, it worked, and all the traders slouched off, suitably peeved, back to their stalls.

To my genuine surprise, the cashiers all clapped and waved with smiles on their faces! As I made my way back to my office, the Italian lady came up to me and said, "Vell done Meester Macloud – Vot they deserved. Now Meester Macloud – I get complimentary theatre and film tickets from my friend – you veel get some next time – you deserve them!" And, bless her, she was as good as her word and, more importantly, we had no more trouble from the street traders!

A RACE TO GET THE FLOUR!

It was just after closing time when a mature lady customer came puffing up to the only checkout open but about to be closed where I, as assistant manager, put through any staff member's shopping. On this particular evening we had workmen in the store and they had started to embark on actions that would save a great deal of time. First we had to move and re-site three whole fixtures of grocery stock items under which the workmen had placed very strong steel poles and were carefully rolling the fittings to their new allotted positions. It was all happening.

"I urgently need some self raising flour," she explained. "I'll be lost without it. Can I please get a couple of packets – I really will appreciate it if you will let me." I looked round and could see the fixture that had the flour she wanted rolling along to its new location. I shouldn't have said it but couldn't resist it … "If you run madam, you'll just catch the fixture with the flour that you want. They're pushing it round the corner." She saw exactly what I meant and set off in pursuit.

She made it and I took her money. Although still

breathless she gasped "Thank you, thank you" and happily trudged off. The unforgettable image of her chasing that fixture still remains with me.

THE OVERALLS ORDER ARRIVED

At last the overalls for the female cashiers and sales floor staff I had long requested had arrived. I opened the parcel to check the count and all seemed fine. On top of this, the new design – pink and white – was most attractive.

I called a number of the girls into the office and gave them the good news and they were naturally delighted. "There is one thing, though," I added -tongue very much in cheek – "I am responsible for them fitting you all just right, so I will have to – er, er – make sure personally that they fit you properly in, er – all parts!" Of course I was saying this anticipating a frosty response, when one young girl burst through the pack, thrust herself forward, and cried "Me first, me first!"

My bluff was well and truly called, and I had to think fast. "I'd love to my dear – but just think of the husbands, boyfriends, and indeed my wife's reaction, when they heard about it!", That said, and in a relaxed and lovely atmosphere, I let them choose their respective new overalls. "Two each, I'm delighted to say, girls." There's nothing picks up the morale of your female staff than new overalls and, yes, I'd learnt a lesson!

Bungling nitwits!

A good friend in a neighbouring store, telephoned and told me he had to get workmen organised to mend a hole in his supermarket roof! Overnight, it seems, two villains had patiently and laboriously drilled a hole – using a pneumatic drill – through part of the roof to allow them to enter and rob the store.

Their hard work, sweat and endeavour was rewarded when finally, after nearly two hours, they penetrated the concrete and made a hole large enough for them to drop through. Sadly for them their pre-planning did not match their physical efforts, because when they dropped through the hole they landed on the pavement of the main street! By this time, even after midnight, they'd been spotted and the local police were waiting! One can only imagine what they must have felt like when they had to explain their actions to the police, drilling through the large overhang part of the roof above the front windows of the store!

KNUCKLING DOWN, DESPITE THE PAIN!

Standing at the back door of my supermarket warehouse in Didcot on a cold windy day was no fun, but I had on this occasion to accept and check in a delivery, since there was no one else to do it. As the driver unloaded my left hand was, for some reason, holding on to the door jamb. Suddenly, the wind blew, and my little finger's knuckle got crushed. The pain was excruciating and I walked round the car park cursing, knowing the bone in my finger had been well and truly broken at the worst possible time.

An hour later I had to go to Oxford to the main hospital where I received the dreaded news that my knuckle was fractured in three places. They put a dressing on it before I made my way back to the supermarket.

At that time we had no clerk to do the administration, so I just had to get on with it and had just cashed the first of five tills, when the area manager paid a surprise visit. As I was in the office, he came to see me and noticed my bandaged hand – left one – I write with my right. I told him what had happened and he immediately said, "Don't work any more today – go home!" Very generous of him, I thought, and asked him who was going to do the cashing up and all the administration. "Are you going to do it?" I was being facetious, well aware he could not do it anyway! I shall, nevertheless, never forget his next comment … "How sore is your finger?" I had a laugh and told him to go away – I'd manage.

My little finger is noticeably deformed to this day – a permanent reminder of this very painful story!

COKE CANS CAN BE LETHAL

I was filling up a metallic display with cans of coke as manager at a Southampton supermarket, when one of the cans was suddenly pierced by a tiny unseen sharp piece of metal on the display bin. The coke sprayed everywhere so I grabbed the can and ran with it through the entrance door before it could do any more damage.

Holding the can away from me and wondering what to do next, I was addressed by a small voice behind me. Two youngsters were sitting on the pavement in front of the supermarket window. One looked at me earnestly and said, "Mister – your can's got a hole in it – take it back, take it back!" Before I could respond he reiterated his advice "Go on, take it back mister!"

However, this coke experience was nothing compared to when a girl dropped a can of coke at closing time. It exploded with its sticky contents going everywhere – on the floor, shelves, and worst of all onto the newly-painted white walls! It took over an hour to clean up the mess but a painter had to redecorate the walls which needed three coats.

HOLE IN THE WALL THEFTS

Managers and head office do not always get it right. At a supermarket in Poole, thieves knocked out the bricks on part of the wall. The hole they created allowed them, without setting off an alarm, to enter the small room that held the tobacco stocks. Around £4,000 worth of cigarettes were stolen and the loss was only discovered the following morning.

CID were involved, but in the meantime builders were contacted and came quickly to reset the bricks – including some matching new ones – into the wall, sealing up the hole. None of us was alert enough to realise how easy it would be for the thieves to knock out the bricks again and remove the remaining new cigarettes stock! No security camera was in place.

The thieves did just that and returned the same night and removed more stock by knocking out the same hole! Although it was suspected this was an inside job, no in-depth interviews or police work took place. You learn by mistakes which can sometimes be very costly.

FROM PENN'S PEN

My friend and fellow manager and supermarket owner, Alan Penn, tells many humorous stories, including about thieving done by old and young alike.

A favourite trick of some farmers who visited a Spar store in the North of Scotland, was to slip a pack of Danish bacon inside their wellington boots. Alan knew how to deal with them though and when the customers came to the till with their newspaper, he would flag up the price of the bacon together with the paper. When the price was queried Alan would say "£1.20 sir for the bacon in your boot". Ironic, when you consider some of them were pig farmers!

Old ladies were, sadly, as guilty as anyone else when it came to stealing. They'd come in with both handles of a carrier bag over their wrist, pick up a basket, and walk slowly round the shop. They'd select a few items but by this time the carrier bag was held by only one handle, making it easy for them to drop in the items they wanted to steal. Many a time I have observed an old person strolling around with say a box of twelve Oxo cubes in their basket and two minutes later – they were gone! Had they put them back? No – usually I could see into the bag, and then told the cashier that I'd serve the potential thief myself. I'd ring up the cat food, for example, and then add the price of the Oxo cubes. They'd query this and I'd reply how I'd come to the charged amount. They just paid and went on their way. I figured it was better to do it this way – or I'd end up banning everyone – and soon end up with no customers – because almost everyone was at it!

Some of my dodgy customers liked to think they were more agile than I was. Sometimes they were correct but often my determination to catch them was enough.

Whilst trading in Worthing one chap came in at various times and initially select a bottle of vodka. It would be placed on the counter and its price rung up on the till. At this moment he'd say, "Oh! I forgot – a packet of Rizla cigarette papers please." This meant that the assistant serving had to turn round to where the cigarettes were displayed to get his request. In a flash he'd grab the vodka and leg it, disappearing into one of the numerous flatlets nearby.

Others tried to emulate this ruse but we were by now ready for it. You learn by experience!

ONE OF OUR OWN DETERRENTS

You had to be more cute than the thieves. Outside one store was a railway line where the barrier came down when trains were imminent in order to stop the traffic. This did not help the shoplifting problem unfortunately, because some of the offenders fleeing from the shop, expertly climbed over the barrier and escaped with their pilfered goods.

It might sound unbelievable but shoplifting was a daily occurrence – or so it felt. We had to do something to deter it and outwit the unscrupulous rogues. We decided that when undesirables were spotted either in the act or behaving suspiciously, whoever witnessed it would call out a phrase that had a "seven" in it, which would be the clue to the location. The thief was also referred to as a "seven".

This proved to be a really successful ploy so if someone called out "Seven packs of bacon, please" a member of staff would know instantly the location to be watched. Equally, if some dodgy person was near the beverages where there were expensive jars of coffee, they would call out, "Seven loaves of bread, please," because the bakery section was next to the fixture with the expensive lines. The thief would look up and think this was just shop talk as bread was not a pilferable item! Staff were always cute enough to understand the call and a number of shoplifters were apprehended through this simple operation.

POLICE – AT THE RIGHT TIME AND PLACE!

One day I was warned by staff there were four yobs acting suspiciously in the store. I followed them wherever they went which they did not like. I felt sure they had nicked something but had not actually witnessed it, so could do nothing but ensure nothing more disappeared. The remarks and personal abuse then began so I asked them to leave and ushered them to the exit.

The shop's doors were made of metal and swung both inwards and outwards but were never a problem. The door swung back and nudged one of the yobs and put him off balance. I was spat on and one took a swipe at me in the scuffle that followed. They were clearly out to cause trouble.

The staff first called the police on the telephone and then had the sense to shout, "Call the police," as matters escalated. This attracted the attention of a car that had stopped at the railway barriers in which were three police officers in plain clothes. They intervened and the yobs ended up being charged with theft and assault. The police were in the right place at the right time – an amazing stroke of luck.

OUR OTHER BRANCH!

I once had a little village store in Wales where I was a bit of a rascal with some of the customers. It was a small shop with a low turnover and profit! Even then, more than 20 years ago, we used to recycle carrier bags – any carrier bag, no matter what name was on it – as long as it was strong enough to make it fit for purpose. We also asked our customers to ensure they brought their own carrier bags and that we'd cheerfully use any of their surplus stock they didn't want!

One day I picked up a carrier bag with Harrods written on it, the posh London store. An old lady came in for some shopping and I put her items into this bag. She paid for her goods and then, as she noticed the name on the side, her brow furrowed a little. I guessed she was puzzled but heard her mutter, "Harrods!". "Yes," I said. "Harrods – that's our other branch." I could swear she muttered, "Hmm, must be doing well ...". Bless her.

THANK YOU BRIAN!

We had to put up with a chap called Brian who had a great liking for the strong cheap cider we sold. He did not drive, so a trip to a supermarket in the nearest town was not for him. Brian visited us frequently, sadly sometimes the worse for wear – under the influence of his booze. Once, when we were busy, he stood near the tills watching the queues come and go. My staff would say, "Thank you" to the customers – and in turn the customers, who appreciated our help and service, would reply, "Thank you," and even add "very much."

Suddenly, Brian left his post and stood at the head of the queue, with his usual purchase in hand. "I don't know," he drawled in a loud voice, "why everyone is saying thank you – at these prices!"

Thank you, Brian!

QUIRKY GOATS MILK

I was a devil at times and liked to kid some of my customers about their purchases. It was harmless fun but perhaps I shouldn't have done it.

As I rang the lady's shopping up on the till I called the prices out loud like, "washing powder £1.20, sugar 69p, etc." When I reached her last item I said, "goat's milk 42p," and handed it to the lady. I then told her the cost of her shopping. "Oh, oh," she exclaimed. "I did not want goat's milk." I asked her if she would put it back in the milk fridge where she got it from and to just take the carton of milk that was next to it.

She duly did this and returned saying, "This is not goat's milk is it?" "No," I said and she went on her merry way. We did not sell goat's milk of course so next time she came in she said to the staff, "And, I don't want goat's milk." Bless her – I genuinely felt guilty at sowing seeds of doubt in her mind.

OUT OF LUCK – YET LUCKY!

We were closed on Christmas Day but open on Boxing Day. Just before I opened up, however, I suddenly remembered I had not changed the CCTV video tapes which only recorded for 24 hours in those days.

Little did I realise this was later to become a big issue. Almost immediately after I opened the door, a chap entered and after a minute or so picked up a whole case of twenty-four cans of lager and walked straight out. Needless to say I went straight after him and approached him. He shouted, "Back off, back off" and turned to run out. He was of course carrying a case of lager and after a few steps he stopped and turned round to face me. In a flash he pulled out a syringe and then lunged at me with it. Luckily the needle did not connect.

I could see he was high on drugs and I quickly made my way back to the store, for once returning empty handed. The police came to see me but alas the CCTV had stopped recording an hour before the incident, so no visual evidence was available. It was unfortunate but, on reflection, I was safe. Somebody lunging at you with a syringe really makes you scared!

THE PINCHING CONTINUED UNABATED!

After taking over a Spar shop in Worthing, it became clear there was a big shoplifting problem. The old couple who had owned it for years had sadly let this side of the business get out of control. So-called customers would walk in, pick up a can, bottle of wine or spirits, a sandwich and some crisps and then simply walk out. We realised that everybody had to be watched – a real challenge – and the last thing you wanted as new owners. However, the hosts of thieves did not realise the business had changed hands since the same sales floor staff were still there. The very first "customer" I followed selected his usual few lines and was just about to step outside the exit door, when he found me blocking the path. A look of frustration and realisation hit him and he about-turned and went back to the till, joined the queue and – as the cashier later began to ring up his "shopping", he suddenly cried, "Oh, I've forgotten my money – keep the stuff – I'll be back." Needless to say he never returned, not that I wanted him to!

We had, by necessity, a pretty decent CCTV system installed, but it wasn't fail-safe. I watched someone take a load of groceries out of the shop without paying. By the time I got to where I reckoned he would be he had vanished. How frustrating is that?! I called the Police and they had a look at the CCTV. Whilst this was going on I noticed through the security glass a lady customer stuffing her large bag with items from the freezer, after she'd made sure no staff were about! The police lady present took off in an instant and the thief was escorted to a waiting police car and taken to the police station

From my office, which was situated in the warehouse, I could still see the sales floor clearly and knew where all the staff were, so it came as a surprise when I heard someone walking softly outside in the warehouse, I was suspicious and stood behind the open door. Incredibly, this unknown person came quietly into the office itself and started looking around. This is what an opportunist thief does of course, and he was undoubtedly looking for the safe or any cash lying around. What a shock he got when I suddenly appeared! "What do you think you are doing here?" I asked him sternly. "Oh, oh, I'm looking for … milk!" he muttered. "Oh, yeah?" I replied, and escorted him out of the store with the, now familiar, warning not to return.

Ironically, somehow a milk carton had been dropped on the floor and was leaking. He'd had to walk past the cabinets to get to where I nabbed him! What a shop! Would the attempted nicking ever stop?

Next day a chap walked in, picked up a can of lager from a stack near the tills and was walking out the door with it when he found me. A few words followed but he wouldn't give up his can of lager. However, the person being served on the till was an off-duty policeman who'd just come off his shift. He heard the commotion and intervened. Producing his warrant card, he told the thief that if he had not been off duty he would have been nicked. He then told him never to come to the shop again. He could not have been more helpful. I was, I realised, trading in an area where many people were often high on drugs, so that may well have been the reason for the amount of attempted and, sadly, successful thieving.

WHAT LENGTHS SOME THIEVES WILL GO TO!

It's not the actual value that a thief gets away with but the damage they are sometimes responsible for.

Outside were two sturdy chewing gum stands. The revenue they took was not great but every little penny helped. It was the middle of summer and thanks to the well-lit main road the explanation for the commotion I heard late in the evening became clear as I looked out from the window. Unbelievably a man was trying to prise the two chewing gum machines from the wall. He was using, unsuccessfully, a garden spade! I shouted at him, "What do you think you are doing?" but by the time I got to the machines he had legged it. He caused some serious damage with his futile efforts and for what? A few pence.

A NICE LITTLE EARNER!

It was a little bit of an issue at the time but it was a nice little earner. We had a notice board in our shop but did not charge much for the postcards people paid to have displayed, the adverts being visible through the window.

Examples of cards on display ...

Mini for Sale: Nice bodywork; regularly serviced; in good working order – phone -----

Or French Polishing – phone -----

I'm afraid quirky ones like the latter were placed by local ladies of the night and the police were forever coming round telling us to remove certain ones from display.

We did as instructed but they were soon replaced by other quirky cards. If we were told to remove them, then we did but the practice went on and on without any comebacks. It stopped eventually but for a time it was a nice little earner!

SEVEN DIALS –
"THE KNOCKER SHOP"!

I lived above the Seven Dials shop in Brighton for a few years. The flat was handily central and there was nothing like the traffic flow there is today. The shop was on the ground floor and the warehouse in a cellar below. My flat was two floors up and had a side entrance from a recessed area about six feet wide, just off the main road.

Attached to the door was a letterbox and a large knocker. The added problem was that both had, in the course of time, become loose and on a windy night the rattling would commence. Not too loud but loud enough to hear as my head hit the pillow at night.

This was bad enough but it was nothing to the continual rattling that would take place on other nights. Many a time, before I took action, I would look out from my bedroom window to see a couple busily engaged but completely oblivious to the consequences of their activities with the prolonged loud rattle of the confounded letter box and knocker! My window was directly above the spot so I decided on a drastic plan of action. I kept a bucket of water handy and when some couple's actions started the knocker rattling, I slid the window fully open and emptied the lot! Sometimes actions speak louder than words and it meant I could at least get the sleep that a hard-working shopkeeper deserved!

CONFUSION OVER GN.

How things have changed in retailing! 40 years ago in at The Seven Dials was when national stores like Tesco were not allowed to sell newspapers or cigarettes. Everyone knew what they were allowed to sell and also what they were not allowed to sell.

There had just been an uproar about a publication called *Gay News* and when it came on to the market some retailers, like W. H. Smith's, refused to stock it. Although it had no indecent content it was displayed on our top shelf! As a small retailer we could not afford to be too choosy about what we sold, and that was that. Then, any shop which sold it displayed a small pink sign in the corner of their shop window. The sign had the initials "GN" on it, to let the public know we stocked it!

When one afternoon a regular customer came into the shop, saw me and said, "I will take a copy of the GN while I am here ...". I promptly went over to the shelves and got one down for him. "60p please", I asked when I got to the till. "What?", he exclaimed, "60p? – it's usually only 22p"

It quickly transpired the gentleman had in fact wanted ... the *Gardening News*!

5 PARK DRIVE

In our little shop we had many customers who benefitted from a delivery system. All the customer accounts were kept in a book we called "The Huggler System", a simple idea with one page for each customer, with weekly payment slips taken out when the week was paid up.

This little shop was busy and we were all serving, when a lady approached our latest inexperienced new recruit and said "5 Park Drive, please." The new girl instantly got hold of the Hugglers account book and, after some desperate thumbing through the book, looked both frustrated and puzzled.

When one of our experienced assistants went over to help it turned out the customer actually wanted five *Park Drive* cigarettes, and pointed to them in the display case. In those days we sold five cigarettes to those who could not afford 10!

THE LOWEST OF THE LOW IN THEFT

During my time as manager in Worthing, I came to the conclusion that the thieves who visited my shop would try almost anything to pinch my stock. They had in no morals or feelings towards shopkeepers – me particularly.

A busy morning was in full flow when a lady suddenly had what appeared to be an epileptic fit. Tins were going everywhere and panic reigned. I told the girl on the till to phone for an ambulance and other customers came to help. The lady was put in the recovery position and covered with a coat but what we did not realise was we were being set up for thieves to remove a sizeable amount of stock while we weren't looking.

Two of the gang were already inside the shop and were simply waiting for the opportunity to remove items when everyone was otherwise engaged. The ambulance soon arrived but, surprisingly, the lady in question had come round and, although she acted in a confused way, she steadfastly refused to go to hospital and happily signed the form that stated that it was at her request she was not taken there.

Then we noticed that all the large jars of coffee were missing and staff began shouting that all the steaks and large joints of meat were missing from the chilled cabinets. We checked the other areas of the shop but they had not been touched. The CCTV was checked but this did not help. Whilst this so-called lady was suffering from an epileptic fit, two experienced thieves had kept their faces covered as they did their business. The police arrived but we had been duped and robbed.

We made a decision and that in the event of any future sudden "illness" we would lock the shop until we were certain it was genuine.

TIME TO MOVE ON

I recall one evening at the same store when a girl and a chap, both around 18 years old, came in. The lad started shoplifting so I decided the best course of action was to approach him and quietly ask him to leave the store, which he did. It was a busy time and customers were queuing, waiting to be served when, without warning, the boy returned and went berserk. I was at the back of the counter when he grabbed the expensive electric scales on the counter and threw it on the floor. It smashed into a thousand pieces, glass flying everywhere. He then went outside and, shouting and swearing, proceeded to boot in and smash the whole plate-glass window. Luckily we had some protection with shelving inside but nevertheless glass, bottles and various grocery lines tumbled from the shelves leaving customers screaming and diving for cover. I pushed the panic button under the counter but noticed the culprit run off in the direction of the railway station.

Within minutes there were police everywhere and I joined them as they toured the area searching for him. Together with a plain clothes policeman, we walked into the busy railway station where I spotted the troublemaker sitting cool, calm and collected, outside the cafe. After I pointed him out, the plain clothes man and another officer, apprehended and handcuffed him. I was pleased that his actions landed him in jail and although he was ordered to pay compensation, we never saw a penny. It was back to the store and the task of clearing up the mess and arranging for the damage, including the plate glass window, to be replaced.

This event put us on high alert but since the store was doing well I decided to invest in extra night staff for security reasons as well as the extra help now required. However, one evening, two men and a woman came into the store around 8pm. All of us, by prior arrangement, split up, and used our now normal warning cry that thieves were about … "Fill the 7UP drinks in the chiller." This simply meant that staff covered the aisle with chilled drinks.

However, the thieves kept a lookout before pinching and if they saw someone near them, would say, "Are you watching me?" We'd reply, "No" but continue attending to the nearby shelf stock and would not move. Often that was enough of a deterrent and a number would simply give up and leave. On this occasion we knew the woman had pinched at least a few soup cans, and she and the others were clearly uncomfortable about our surveillance as they left the store. I followed, and as they got into their van I wrote down its number plate so I'd have something in the event of their quick getaway. The woman, after seeing me noting their number, jumped out of the van, slapped me on the face and spat at me. As they drove off, a number of cans came flying through the air in my direction and a couple were thrown at the store's window. Luckily the tins hit the brick wall under the glass so no damage was incurred.

We considered the incident and decided not to report it since they could return later and if we took this action they might leave us alone. Thankfully, they never returned but this continual battle against thieves was getting to me. The final straw, as the owner of the store, was when the news reached me that a chap with a shotgun was raiding all the garages, post offices and grocery stores in the area, and that his raids now totalled ten. He even had the cheek to rob the same garage twice in the same day. I have wondered occasionally if, on seeing how many extra male staff I'd employed particularly to work in the evenings this had deterred him from adding us to his list. I will never know but he may well have thought my store was a little too risky. The police had an ongoing undercover operation, with shops that were likely targets being kept under surveillance. We were told they even had armed response units at the ready.

However, enough was enough and I put the store up for sale and moved on. It was a scary and dangerous time of my life.

OH! WHAT A SURPRISE

We all know that health workers in hospitals and care homes have certain nose-twitching duties to perform from time to time but I'll bet nobody guesses that food store managers also occasionally have to clean up similar human mess. One Saturday afternoon about 2pm a regular customer – an old lady I had got to know – came to the till in a flustered state and a great hurry. She plonked a one pound coin on the counter and cried "This is for the jar of strawberry jam" and fled out of the door. I tidied up the till and made my way into the shop floor area, where, immediately, I caught a whiff of a horrible pungent odour. I ventured forward a few steps and the source of the vile smell was on the floor in front of me. With the help of an assistant, we set to and cleared away the mess and spread disinfectant and diluted bleach over the area. Job done we raced outside for fresh air!

As luck would have it later that same day, a lady shopper's child suddenly vomited all over the same area we had just cleared up! The woman abandoned her shopping trip and took the child outside, leaving us to clean up again! It was not pleasant but not as bad as the previous job. Once again, I departed outside afterwards to breathe in some much needed fresh air!

There is a saying that things happen in threes and it really did on this particular day! At 7.30pm I locked up and set the alarm but the very second I stepped outside, a passing drunk stumbled, fell and accidentally punched me in the face. Next day I had a reminder of this third unfortunate incident – a lovely black eye.

CAUGHT WITH THEIR
TROUSERS DOWN!

Near my store in Worthing was a busy and popular brothel in one of the terraced houses. The madams and their helpers often frequented my store and spent very good money. Trouble was, ethically, it was someone else's money because clients were asked to leave their clothes in a separate room to where the men booked in before disappearing inside for their pleasure. Whilst there, however, a female gang would remove the clients' credit cards. In an era where the zip zap machines processed cards without authorisation for anything under £100, this is what happened next. The maids would quickly practise the signature on the card and then nip round to the SPAR (us!) and buy various purchases, including lottery tickets. Sales were always in excess of £50, quite a lot at that time. They would then hurry back to the brothel and replace the cards in the wallets or pockets, and resume their normal duties.

The client meanwhile would pay his fee, and a month later he'd get his credit card statement, which would include various payments to us! They would ask their bank for the reason for charges and would subsequently write to us. We'd send a copy of the sales docket and would never hear another word! They realised they'd been unfortunately caught, as it were, "with their trousers down!"

A KEYMAN? NOT ME!

One particular store offered a service that was surprisingly popular – key cutting. It was a service I had to learn, however, before the dreaded day arrived when I had to cut my first key. It was just before a Bank Holiday and a new machine had replaced the old one when a lady customer asked if I could cut two Yale keys which she wanted to give to friends coming to stay. Simple? Not as it turned out.

I placed the original key in a small clamp on the left hand side and placed a blank key on the right. A precision cutting wheel replicated the key which I then put in a vice and used a wire brush to remove any rough edges.

Most customers would try out their new key when they returned home, and 99% of the time everything was fine. However, on this occasion the lady did not do this but simply gave them to her friends as quickly as possible. A few days later she returned and berated me because one of the keys did not fit properly and her friend had snapped it in the lock, causing havoc.

Now I knew the key had been copied accurately and that both copies had been perfect, so why had one failed?

After some discussion she admitted the guest had returned the worse for drink and under the influence had snapped the key in the lock. If the customer had checked both keys then the subsequent problem of the demon drink would have been avoided.

On another occasion a different nightmare occurred. I cut a Yale key and gave the copy to the customer. Within an hour she was back saying the copied key did not fit properly which sometimes happened if the lock was old and worn, as was the case in this instance. A bit rattled, I set out to cut another replacement but got the keys muddled up and placed the faulty key on the left, where the original should have been. As a result, I ensured that neither key would now fit or open the lock! Fortunately, after ringing her landlord I was able to obtain a spare key which was sent to the shop by taxi – which I had to pay for!

ALL'S WELL THAT ENDS WELL

Imagine a very cold, snowy night in the north of Scotland. That's how it was when I was duty manager of a supermarket with three hard-working lassies in my store. The snow began to fall heavily as 8pm approached and, in fairness to them and myself – all of whom had quite a distance to get home – I decided to close the store a little earlier than 9pm. There had been no customers in the half an hour prior to normal closing time and I felt justified in my decision so I set the alarm and we left to make our snowbound way home.

As soon as I opened up next morning I received a telephone call from head office. I had risen and left home at 4.20am, deliberately taking the long way round because the usual road had not been very well gritted. Despite opening up early head office bawled me out for shutting early the previous night! A local customer had visited the store five minutes before normal closing time to get her fags and head office knew when we left because of the alarm timing and were simply not interested in the atrocious local weather conditions.

Deflated, as I put the phone down, I thought I spied a cat at the top of the stairs leading to the upstairs stock room. On inspection I found a beautiful white cat with two new kittens! She had somehow got into this rather dilapidated office by climbing up the wall and entering through an old air vent. She now wanted to leave but a very cold and snowy morning awaited her if we allowed it so we gave her some cat food which was hungrily received. One of the staff lived on a farm and offered to give the kittens a new home. However, she was quickly also drawn to the cat and in the end all three found a new warm home.

Looking back it was a rewarding conclusion to a day that had started so badly and the weather conditions improved too.

FUEL FOR FREE!

Back in the 1970s my family had an old fashioned hardware store that sold everything from pots and pans to loose nails and cutting keys. We also sold pink paraffin, which lots of people used for various hearing appliances. In the rear storage room we kept a rusty old metal tank that held 500 gallons of paraffin, our entire stock.

On the forecourt was a self-service paraffin pump that customers could use during the weekends and evenings when we were closed – very popular during the cold winter months. It was a good earner when a gallon cost just 37 pence! A paraffin storage tank inside a shop with flats above would fill today's health and safety officials with horror but that's how it was!

On delivery day we turned the tank off so it could fill up and afterwards turned it back on as it operated on gravity and would be slow to fill any containers. The tank, which was on a framework, was high off the ground and its gravity control was manually operated from within the shop.

One day the delivery arrived late. It was bitterly cold and the shop was busy which was our only excuse for what happened after we forgot to switch the tank back on. It was a costly mistake because as soon as folk discovered they could put as little as 1p into the slot to receive a gallon of paraffin, the machine's popularity increased no end!

The next morning, when we were opening up, one of the ladies who lived in the flats above the shop remarked, "The paraffin machine has been extra busy during the night – probably due to the very cold weather. Still it's good to see you getting the trade."

When we emptied the machine's takings we were in for a terrible shock. To our horror we found the actual takings were only £6.74 but over 400 gallons had been withdrawn by a number of very grateful and surprised customers, who obviously passed the word around! We were out of pocket by £150 – a great deal of money in those days!

WATER, WATER, EVERYWHERE!

In one store we were frequently asked if we knew any tradesmen or handymen who could do basic repair jobs around the home. You know the sort of thing – paint a room, or fix a lock, etc. and some tradesmen left their calling cards with us which we were happy to hand them out to customers who could then make direct contact. However, it occurred to me that if we employed our own handyman on a part-time basis, we could have a profit-sharing agreement with him. It was a little ambitious but seemed like a good idea so we employed a chap called Mick and the jobs began to roll in. He was a jack the lad, always full of stories which the customers loved to hear and could turn his hand to most things in the days when there were few trade union restrictions on what you could – or could not do.

Mr. and Mrs. Nichols needed their gutters cleared and Mick, with all his charm, was just the man. He arrived with a long ladder and got to work, soon completing a tidy job. He was just leaving when Mr. Nichols asked him to check on a job previously done by someone else. A shock awaited him when he looked in the attic, however, where a large plastic sheet had been laid across the beams below the roof, on top of which he could see a large amount of water, the result of some crooked roofers who had charged him £300 for a bodged job.

Mick realised he had to empty the loft of water before any new tiling could be started so pushed a hosepipe under the eaves which started a trickle. In the meantime Mrs, Nichols, who was frail and walked with a zimmer frame, decided to investigate what was going on and slowly made her way along the side of the house and looked up to see the water trickling through the pipe. Unfortunately she moved too close, just as Mick lifted the sheet to prompt a greater flow of water from the hose. It worked and the unfortunate Mrs. Nichols, who could only move very slowly, got absolutely drenched before she could move a muscle. Her daughter luckily lived nearby and, hearing the cries for help, popped over to help her mum into a warm shower and a change of clothes.

A JOKE FROM UNEXPECTED QUARTERS!

One day I was telling a joke to a member of staff, one of those about a Scotsman, Englishman and Irishman but was unaware a regular customer was listening, a fellow who usually had a serious facial expression. He was about to leave, but turned round quite unexpectedly and said in his usual, almost gloomy manner ...

"Did you hear about the Scotsman who was heading out of his house to the pub? As he was about to leave he turned to his wee wife and said, 'Jackie, put your hat and coat on lassie.' She replied, 'Aw Ian, that's nice – are ye taking me to the pub with you?' "Naw," was the reply, "I am just switching the central heating off while I'm oot!"

SERVING ONE OF THE GREATS

Around 1979 in Brighton I acquired my very own little fresh fruit and vegetable shop. I also sold bouquets of loose flowers. It was situated quite close to the Theatre Royal and I used to stay open on Sundays until 5pm, something which not many others did. However, I found that Sunday trading had the hidden benefit of being able to clear lines that would otherwise be thrown out on the following Monday.

On one unforgettable Sunday afternoon, I was tidying up when a well-dressed gentleman came in whom I greeted with, "Good afternoon, Sir." He replied, "Yes, it's a good one." I then asked how I could help. He replied "I would like to buy a bouquet of flowers for my leading lady, please."

To this I casually replied, with a little smile, "Is it your wife's birthday, sir?" He laughed. It was a laugh that no one else could ever copy, and he said, "No, No – I am at the theatre and this is my last day when I always treat my leading lady to flowers!" It was only then that he actually told me his name ... Norman Wisdom!

I hadn't recognised him, yet he had been my hero when I was growing up. It suddenly all came back, his stature and just the way he was, Norman Wisdom, ... I felt in awe but this quickly disappeared as we began to chat, as he went on to tell me about all the musical instruments he played, adding a couple of theatrical stories as well.

I just couldn't get over how talented he was. I slowly put together the very best bouquet I could, and confess I robbed my Monday flower orders in the shop to do it, so he got the very best that I had. I felt this was going to be a unique moment in my life – and it was. I had met my theatrical hero who turned out to be an absolute gem of a man, who had given me his time for a perfect chat.

I handed the bouquet over and he was clearly pleased with it. He proffered a couple of notes but, although I couldn't really afford it, I declined the money and found the words to tell him it was but a small gesture from me in return for the many laughs and entertainment he'd given me down the years. For just a moment he seemed touched, and then, with that famous grin, he left my little shop. As he walked away he raised his hand and gave me a little wave. The memory still brings a lump to my throat as I recall it.

A JOB THAT WENT WRONG

One of my customers called Pam asked us to arrange for someone to fix a pipe that was leaking in her ceiling above the kitchen. It was a rubber push pop connection hose rather than copper piping and it later transpired someone had moved it, only slightly but enough to cause a slight leak.

Everyone was oblivious to the lurking problem until one day Pam, a wonderful cook, was busy at her stove cooking dinner for some foreign students who lodged with her, when the disaster occurred. Water from the leak had been absorbed into the plasterboard until the added weight brought the whole ceiling crashing down, resulting in a great deal of noise and confusion. Luckily no one was hurt but the mess was something to behold. The insurers paid up but the ever resilient Pam blamed herself, with her final words on the subject being "The dinner was ruined!"

She was an unforgettable and unsinkable customer!

JUST A REFLECTION

When my parents ran a newsagents shop in Brighton, I learned a little bit of my trade there but what I recall the most is that we had no burglar alarms and no CCTV because robberies were few and far between. So different to how it is today and although one shouldn't look back it was indeed a different era … very different to many other stores I managed.

NOTHING TO BE ALARMED ABOUT!

It was 4.45am and I was making my way as normal to my village store in Wales, where I always checked the street was safe and drove with my car headlights on. I opened the door of the store, entered and went to turn the alarm off at the control box but for some reason I keyed in the wrong code, panicked and re-entered it. Unbeknown to me I had keyed in the distress code in error but satisfied the alarms were now off, I carried on with my usual routine of putting the papers on display and marking up all the papers ready for delivery to customers. I usually worked by the light of the chillers as the shop was not yet open. The rear stockroom light however still shone through to the shop floor area.

At about 5.10am I heard a loud banging on the front glass door which scared me but I went over to where a chap was standing by an unmarked police car parked outside. After shouting "Police", held up his warrant card and told me to open the door and asked if all was OK? I said, "Yes", but then two more plain clothes police entered – both armed! My mistake was obvious but they insisted on searching the entire premises and also outside in case I was being held against my will.

It was a scary moment but I felt reassured about the protection that was on hand from the local police. I made sure I never got the system wrong again!

BAD LEG

I charged as much as I dared for most products because making a profit is essential for all private traders to survive. One day I was limping because my leg was painful when a regular lady customer noticed and said "Alan, have you hurt your leg, dear?"

My reply was: "No, Ethel … it's just our crippling prices!" I always tried to give the customers a smile – if not cheaper prices!

WHAT CHANCE HAVE THEY GOT?

In my village shop in Wales I was a jack of all trades but while busy doing a variety of tasks in the warehouse, I spotted two teenage boys leaning over the counter, trying to open one of the tills. Fortunately it was locked so I made myself known and asked them what they were doing. They were, however, unperturbed and, with a cocky air, replied casually with a shrug of the shoulders, "Looking at the till."

I told them to leave and not to return but two hours later an irate woman appeared demanding to know why I had banned her boys from the shop. I described what happened and that it was actually on our CCTV which she was welcome to watch. I added that I was happy for the police to see it too, if that was what she wanted.

Once she saw her "lovely boys" had tried to rob her local shop I mistakenly thought she would change her aggressive behaviour. Not a bit of it! She assumed a haughty, arrogant look and, with a toss of her head, strode out of the shop without a further word.

If that was how the parent of the boys behaved after

seeing irrefutable evidence of their attempted robbery then what chance was there for them?

It was time for a cup of tea and less reflection.

NEARLY UNHINGED

New Year is not a good time for a potential disaster to occur in a shop but it did. At 7pm I was ready to go home and, with everything attended to, put my key in the lock of the heavy metal door and set the alarm. I was closing it when completely unexpectedly the top hinge snapped, leaving it swinging perilously on the bottom hinge. Meanwhile, the alarm was counting down.

Panic! Somehow I managed to push the door back into a stable position and rushed to cancel the alarm but now what? There was no chance of getting anyone to carry out the repairs so I reset the alarm and took a chance by manipulating the door into its normal position so the alarm would go off if somebody touched it. If anybody had done, it would have immediately swung open and possibly fallen down but it was a risk I had to take despite the potential access to so much stock inside.

Thankfully nothing further happened, and I got it repaired after three days. Meantime, we had to keep it open in the bitter cold during the day, with the help of a heavy fire extinguisher jammed up against it! Despite this, customers still kept trying to shut it. We were all perma-nently cold but had to stay open, an event which nearly left me "unhinged".

UNFORGETTABLE – THAT'S WHAT IT WAS

In retirement you reflect on the best and worst store you ever worked in. In my case the store I chose had the same address! How could this be?

It was the 6th of January, when I reported to take up my first appointment as manager with the new company. I had never actually seen the store so had no idea what it looked like but had to meet the company's training officer there at 8am. I was both nervous and keen but ready to take on any retailing challenge! Good thing too.

Believe it or not, it was an old railway carriage which had been converted into a shop! It was old and rotten, both inside and out and as one walked from one end to the other the floor was so loose that due to vibrations some of the stock would fall from the shelves.

I could not believe what I'd let myself in for but thankfully the young training officer was a wonderful teacher. She was so patient, and painstakingly explained to me the world of good old fashioned paper ledgers and so forth. No computers in those days! It was the era I was born into and so far had thrived in. No scanning items at the till where everything was priced by sticky tickets issued from a big pricing gun!

In the course of my first day I was taught all the essential things I had to do and as I was enthusiastic and keen to do well I listened to the advice and made valuable notes as well. Finally, I felt confident and ready! It then transpired the old carriage had recently been acquired by SPAR's head office but it was also revealed that a brand new store was to be built next door and that the old railway carriage would soon close with all the stock transferred to the new one – my store! Six times larger than the old one and built to SPAR's new plans it was to be a model for other stores to follow. Exciting times lay ahead!

My big moment arrived and on my first day in the railway carriage I was handed the keys. It was my own branch and I still recall how proud I felt. My instructions were to sell off all the old stock at reduced prices, including items such as mothballs, candles, shoe whiteners, etc., all from a bygone era. It was imperative that I cleared as much as possible but I became concerned when I learnt that only modern products would be sold in the new store, with many older lines discontinued, such as those loved by the locals, including pearl barley and yellow split peas which were very popular and used for making the local broth – so beloved in this rural area. My fears of a backlash were soon proved justified but, fortunately, the area manager had lived in the area all his life and recognised that a speedy change of direction was required. Happily, we received permission to restock some of the old lines which kept the customers extremely content.

Four new staff were employed and trade took off in a new learning curve for all. A special re-opening was held with all the staff in their new uniforms plus myself in a blazer and tie, all photographed for the press and SPAR journal! There was even a local radio celebrity who opened the store, with pictures appearing in the local paper which included myself standing alongside the "star", under the banner headline "SPARRING PARTNERS". It was a great success and the sales figure brilliant, our takings for Thursday, Friday and Saturday exceeding what the company thought we might take in a week!

The store looked stunning and our high standards were the talk of the town, with SPAR headquarters inviting other SPAR traders to visit us. Many did and were suitably impressed, and envious.

OH, WHAT A BEAUTIFUL MORNING!

Every store has to check the cash contents of the till each day and ensure that net contents balance with the figure on the audit roll. If that does not happen it can be a problem and was always a stressful time. One morning I checked the first two tills at 5am which were both very accurate despite good takings. However, the third till produced a different picture altogether and was £400 short.

I trusted my staff who exhausted all the avenues of potential loss but to no avail. In this store when the cashiers had a lot of notes they inserted them into a small tube, labelled with the till number and put it into the floor safe via a chute. A normally safe, secure and reliable system.

Determined to find the reason for the loss, I noticed that a small waste bin normally situated close by had been removed and wondered why. Investigation was clearly needed and I was overjoyed that my intuitive mind proved to be right. Now in a new location, there was the rubbish bin and the £400 neatly banded, sitting on top of it ready for disposal! It was a genuine accident but it could have ended very differently! "Oh what a beautiful morning" has never been sung more spontaneously or lustily than my rendition that morning!

TIME TO GO

Every time I watch *The Vicar of Dibley* on television, I think of the first episode when the Rev. Pottle proved in his old age susceptible to nodding off, until the time finally came when Alice gently touched his arm when he was seemingly in his reflective thinking position in the pulpit, and the old chap fell off. His gaffer had called him to his celestial home.

Well, it wasn't *that* bad but I did have a 76 year old who used to sit on a stool in front of the cigarettes and served the public for many years. Sadly, her age caught up with her, and she too began to doze and I had to keep an eye on her in case she fell off the stool. She was a dear, loyal soul but it was time she retired, a hard task to have to undertake but one which I dealt with very discreetly. We looked after her financially of course and she left surrounded by bouquets and chocolates. We all shed a few tears.

NOW...
MORE TALES
FROM COLIN'S
COLLECTION

LUNCH BREAK WITH
A SHOWBIZ LEGEND

The Swanage supermarket had received a massive makeover. New refrigeration had been installed, new features, and new tills. Redecoration had taken place throughout and on top of this the company had arranged for Leslie Crowther to help promote the re-launch. He arrived mid-morning and was well received by the many shoppers, having assured me earlier that a salad lunch would be just fine. This was duly organised and at midday I sat down at a table in the office with Leslie Crowther, and the most genial of Scots, the company's wines and spirits director, Alistair Weatherstone. The normally fairly reserved Alistair proved an absolute revelation.

"I saw you, Mr Crowther," he began, "… when you first appeared in the Fol de Rols variety group at Edinburgh. Do you remember those days?" "I do, I do," replied Leslie. The reminiscing which followed was quite fascinating, with Leslie going back to 1957 at Scarborough, Glasgow and

Aberdeen, where he worked with such household names as Arthur Askey, Elsie and Doris Waters, Jack Warner and others.

Alistair proved to be one of the most informed theatre buffs I'd ever met, and this served to prompt memory after memory from our celebrated guest, who'd presented the *Black and White Minstrel Show* in his time. As somebody who'd listened to the *Ovaltineys Show* on Radio Luxemburg, I'd never guessed that Leslie had been part of it. He'd appeared in a Royal Variety performance and on TV so many times in *Crackerjack* and *The Price is Right*.

For some reason the conversation turned to family life and a discussion on things like weddings of sons and daughters. Leslie had us chuckling when he quipped "When Phil Lynott of the group *Thin Lizzy* asked me for my daughter's hand in marriage, I said to him, "Why not? You've had everything else!" Because he clearly trusted us, he revealed quite a number of secrets and the off-stage personas of household names – all of which amazed us but which will remain secret.

Sadly, both Leslie Crowther and Alistair died only a handful of years later but that couple of hours was an episode I'll always treasure.

STAYING STRONG

And there she was, this rotund, short lady, crouched low popping grocery items into her holdall instead of into her shopping basket. I'd just descended the stairs at the supermarket in Earls Court, and this was the scene before me, although she was clearly unaware of my presence. I stood motionless and watched as she made her way to the till. Earls Court supermarket was small and sometimes congested, both on the sales floor and at the tills, but I could see the items in her holdall had neither been produced nor rung up.

She left the store but I managed to squirm through the queues and reach the pavement, where I asked if she would come back into the store since I believed she'd left without paying for some items. She nodded and I turned to lead the way – or so I thought – to the entrance but when I turned round she wasn't there! I was horrified – where had she gone? She had actually bored her way back onto the sales floor by squeezing past customers causing obvious inconvenience. I espied her on the sales floor, however, and guided her to the downstairs office nearby.

I then explained to the boss that "This lady has left without paying for items in her bag," and, without actually seeing them again, named two or three of the items. She loudly denied that she had done this, inviting the store manager to take a look inside her bag. It was empty except for a couple of items she had actually paid for. My eyes must have been saucer-like as I, in turn, exclaimed, "It's empty". Then, looking at her accusingly, I said, "I clearly saw you put things in your bag. You didn't pay for them before you left, so where have you put them?"

She categorically denied she'd taken anything, stating it in a cold calculated way. The manager was not supportive at this point, muttering, "It looks like you've made a mistake, Colin". At that point she returned to the attack with, "I want an apology – a written apology, signed, right now!" You can imagine my response! It was an emphatic, "No. We both know what you did but where the goods are now I don't know. But apologise? For what?" "Right!" she replied. "I'm going to put this in the hands of my solicitors."

I retraced my footsteps with the manager in tow immediately she left and we quickly found the products she had stolen, rammed between a magazine rack and the side of the till. The manager asked the cashier where they'd come from who said she hadn't seen them until a fat woman pushed her way past her queuing customers. I looked at the boss. "Game, set and match" I said. He agreed and put the items in a bag and kept them in his office.

Incredibly, after an hour the woman returned, demanding

to see the boss and myself. She plonked a large thick photograph album on his desk and rapped out, "You don't know who I am, do you? Well, I'll tell you." She then named one of the biggest names in showbiz, a singer, comedian, entertainer and presenter on TV, who has remained in the public eye right up until today. Out of respect for both this lady, who has now passed on, and to this nationally known figure, I'll refrain from naming him. She added, "That's who I am – and I'll prove it." She opened up the album to start revealing photos taken of her with this famous star, along with people like Princess Margaret etc. "Now," she said triumphantly. "You know who I am and you will realise why I am demanding a written apology." She glared at me but, with my integrity at stake, I replied, "Madam, I couldn't care less who you are. I know exactly what you did and you know what you did. No matter what, I am not apologising to you, and that's that!". We stared at each other like two combatants. She rose, grabbed her album and said, "Right. You'll be hearing from my solicitors." After she left, the boss was both subdued and worried because he had to report the situation to head office.

Two days later a top executive and the area manager arrived and I was told to report to the office. Without ado I was informed the company had received a letter from the star's solicitors, requesting, not only an apology, but indicating they would also sue, stating "defamation of character." "We want you to agree to let her have the written apology and that hopefully will be the end of the matter." My reply was a quick one. "No. I am not going to do that. The manager, myself and the cashier know what the woman did. She knows that I know what she did. Therefore, no matter what, I am not apologising." They looked stunned. They'd leaned heavily on me, but I refused to have my integrity compromised.

I left the office and made my way down the stairs to the sales floor. I felt let down and miserable. Now, I had never before had an alcoholic drink at work but this was the exception. I nipped out to the pub next door. "Give me a double whisky," I said to the barman and in less than a minute it was paid for, downed, and I was back inside the shop. Goodness – I now had a warm glow inside me and felt much better! Passing me was the head office executive on his way out of the store. I smiled at him warmly but my smile wasn't acknowledged. Nevertheless I was pleased I'd done it! When they had gone the boss felt I was doomed and a phone call later that afternoon told me to report to Ruislip head office at 9am on Monday morning, which further confirmed his worst fears. He didn't want to lose me but he felt I was destined for the sack.

That weekend was a long one but I prepared myself mentally for what was possibly going to happen. Sitting before me on Monday morning was the company's security director, personnel director and the managing director himself. It was the latter who leaned forward on his curved glass-topped desk, looked me straight in the eye and said, in a heavy voice, "Well, young man, I expect you are sitting here this morning feeling very worried." There was a silent pause.

I answered in a clear strong voice. "No, I am not sitting here this morning before you as a worried young man and when I go to my next company I shall tell them exactly what happened. I saw someone leave my company's store with shopping she had not paid for. When I went outside to ask her to come back I never considered my own personal position, or that if it went wrong it would damage my career prospects. No, for me it was a clear case of shoplifting but she managed to get rid of the evidence before I got her to the office, and I am not the only one who has been caught out this way. Even the security lady who normally walks the sales floor, asked a lady in similar circumstances to come back and go with her to the upstairs office. She led the way and the lady followed. When they reached the office and her bag was opened, the goods in question were not there. It later transpired the shoplifter had dropped the items over the banister on her way up the stairs! No, I am not worried and will also tell my next company that I've worked for you for three years and gone everywhere I've been asked to, and maintained a good record with each manager. That's what I shall tell my next company."

Three pairs of eyes stared unblinkingly at me. There was another pause when no one said a word. The managing director spoke and simply said "Wait outside Mr. MacLeod." A few minutes later the security director appeared and said, "We want you to return to Earls Court and tell the manager, Mr. King, to get down here straight away." When I walked into the store he was genuinely surprised to see me and after I gave him the message, although still puzzled, he gave me the store keys and made his way to head office.

About an hour later the butcher raced past me on the sales floor on his way towards the tills, yelling at me, "She's got my meat. She's got my meat. She's done it before" and, with that he was disappearing through the exit door. I was after him in a flash! I was in enough trouble already but simply had to catch him before he reached the customer. Outside the store it was like a scene from an old Benny Hill show, as I frantically chased after him. Too late! Not only had he physically stopped her but he'd lost the plot and was waving his finger in her face shouting, "You've got my meat, I know you have!"

The customer accused was tallish, dark-haired, quite good looking and in her thirties. I stepped in – I had to. As I restrained the butcher, I had a real bit of luck. The top of the large holdall she was carrying partially opened and I could see some red packs of fresh meat wrapped in cellophane. The adrenalin in me was flowing. "Madam," I said firmly. "All the cashiers in my store have firm instructions to put those packs of meat into brown paper bags because these packs are inclined to leak blood. So which cashier let you leave these packs not wrapped as they should be. Tell me please?" I maintained a concerned, serious countenance and looked her straight in the eye.

She lowered her gaze and uttered the words I shall never forget. "I'll pay. I'll pay." I replied "We can't sort this out here, so let us get into the office – now" and led the way with the becalmed and thankfully silent butcher behind her. A shock awaited us. Not only had she left with a stack of meat but other expensive items as well, and she could do nothing but admit that she'd not paid for them either. We all sat down and the amount attempted to be stolen reached a staggering £200 plus, a huge amount in the 1960s.

I told the butcher to stay put whilst I used another telephone. If a shoplifter was caught, we had to phone head office security to get the authority to prosecute. I asked to speak to the security director but was told by the girl on reception "He's in a meeting in the managing director's office." I explained to her precisely what their meeting was about and to tell him it was me who wanted him. When he came to the telephone I told him I'd caught a shoplifter. "You what?", he yelled down the telephone. "You what?" I calmed him down and told him the good news. "Prosecute" he said, "and let me have a report of the details." An hour later Mr. King, the manager, returned and beckoned me over. "The managing director has told me to inform you that they will not sack you if it costs £10,000, and that they will be writing to this huge star's solicitors and tell them to take us to court, because there will be no apology from us. We'll see them in court!"

I was overjoyed. I could scarcely believe it but also admired the courage of the managing director in taking the course of action. Now was the waiting game and in less than a week I was informed the star's solicitors had informed the company they no longer wished to pursue the matter – it was dropped. My unyielding fight to get the truth revealed and to protect my integrity had been successful. All I wanted now was to resume my assistant manager's duties as normal with no other worries. That, however, was not going to happen.

A few days later I opened the manager's mail on his day off and out popped a list of the company's stores, their managers and assistant managers. Out of interest I scanned the list. To my surprise I saw the same name as myself at the company's flagship store in Harrow but my name was also against Earls Court – strange! Coming from Scotland everyone in London called me "Jock" and I couldn't resist making a call to head office just to receive confirmation that there were two "J. MacLeods" working for the company. "Oh, dear," the receptionist exclaimed – "Have you not seen anybody from personnel in the last 24 hours?" "No," I replied. "Ah! Well Colin, you will, and the news will be good – you've been promoted! I'll amend the Earls Court entry and send another list out."

From the depths of despair to the giddy heights in less than a couple of weeks! Believe it or not, I did spare a thought for the national treasure of the entertainment world, as I joyfully skipped out of the store that night. After all, he'd simply acceded to his grandmother's wishes (or demands). Whether or not he would have minded the fact that I'd borrowed a well-known song from his industry, rearranged the words slightly, and sang it all the way home is another matter, but it seemed to me to somehow fit the moment ... "There's no business like store business, there's no business I know ...".

A SQUARE PEG IN A ROUND HOLE

"I wonder if you could do something for me?" It was the voice of the managing director on the telephone, speaking on a private line. "Of course", I replied. " How can I help?" "Well, this is a little embarrassing actually but a past associate of mine has asked if I can give him the chance to learn about supermarketing with a view to him taking a fast-track to management. He's in his mid-forties and has been in business for a number of years, but unfortunately not successfully. I know you'll do your best, which is why I am asking you but be aware the chap has various issues, can be difficult and, frankly, if it turns out to be too difficult, please contact me alone. There'll be no wage charge against your store. Just do your best." I assured him that I would. Some people applied directly to head office for a job opportunity – frequently failed undergraduates – but this was different.

Alex Lumpkin arrived the following day at around 9am, late for anyone starting out in supermarkets. He told me how bad luck had played a big part in the failure of his clothing company and that he was simply here because he wanted to know more about the supermarket industry, management in particular. He was not making the right noises but I said I felt he should make a start by learning the basics in the meat department. "Well, my religion won't allow me to touch pork or bacon! Certain things are therefore taboo for me."

I had given my assurance to the managing director and, irrespective of his misgivings, left him in the charge of the meat department manager who asked Lumpkin to watch the other butcher using the mincing machine. When he finished he took Lumpkin to the storage refrigerator and asked him to pop some meat in the mincer while he went upstairs for his tea break. It was a simple enough instruction but Lumpkin turned his attention instead to the attractive lady whose job was pre-packing the meat and poultry. She had to remind him he was expected to have finished the mince by the time the butcher returned. It transpired he was more interested in concluding his conversation than getting the meat out of the refrigerator to mince, but in the end he did it and popped it in the mincer. The result was some beautiful red mince on the empty tray, so job done.

The butcher returned and gazed at the tray but after a glance at the smiling Lumpkin, his face took on a serious expression and he made his way to the refrigerator. He returned in a towering rage. In his hands was a smallish quantity of meat. "You blithering fool" he raged, "You've gone and minced all our fillet steak. Apart from the fact you've cost us money, we've customers who'll be coming in for it. Why the heck were you not more careful?" Lumpkin was shaken and muttered "Sorry, just a mistake."

In the next two days the butcher attempted to teach him how to bone beef, but Lumpkin's concentration was poor and his knife control potentially lethal. "Sorry boss, but he's either going to hurt himself or somebody passing him. He shouldn't have a knife in his hand and so far as him being interested in my meat department – forget it. You must take him out of it – now."

Lumpkin was next on the fresh fruit and vegetables section. The manager was called Gordon and the spitting image of "Blakey" on the TV sitcom *On the Buses*. He was not happy about Lumpkin but said he'd do his best. There were two scales on the unit and 50% of the stock on sale was loose, requiring to be weighed and priced. Gordon caught me on my own on the shop floor after just one day ... "He's a lazy sod. He just will not rotate the fruit or vegetables he has to replenish. He thinks I don't notice but I do and he just shrugs. He also avoids serving customers as if it's beneath him." "Give him another day, Gordon, and don't be afraid to lean on him" I replied.

Later that day I heard a couple of shouts from the fruit and veg area. Lumpkin had been given the job of topping up the loose orange display but had taken a short cut and instead of placing each orange carefully on top of the next one, had tipped the last contents of the box on the display, thus over-filling it drastically. A lady shopper with a basket took one orange off the display and an avalanche of oranges had not only filled her basket but peppered the poor lady bodily. Lumpkin, seeing the disaster, leapt forward towards her to see what he could do but sadly stood on an orange and fell heavily against the fitment. As a result he caused another avalanche of fruit, this time apples. Pandemonium reigned and, when Gordon, alias Blakey, reappeared, his face was a picture. As he stomped into my office I said "I can guess what you're going to say and the answer is 'yes'. Sorry mate, I know you didn't want him. Well you don't have him any more."

Things were now getting pretty dire. If I could only keep him a couple of weeks before giving up, that would be something. What to do? I thought if I placed him on the grocery sales floor and gave him something to fill up, (that he couldn't possibly damage) it would be a temporary answer. Breakfast cereals! That was it – he could fill them up ...

At this particular supermarket in Denmark Hill, South London, all the grocery stock was in the warehouse above the sales floor and to get it down you had to place the cases on an elevator belt. There was a stop and go button at the top of the belt, which ran parallel to the stairs but it was necessary, indeed vital, to leave a couple of feet between the items on the belt to facilitate the unloading. All this was explained to Lumpkin, who clearly indicated by his bored expression, that the instruction was unnecessary. I had forgotten, of course to mention something else that was important but didn't realise it at the time.

After an hour, a female assistant came over to me and said, "Mr MacLeod. I've got to tell you. There's going to be an accident. It's that plonker Lumpkin. You'd better go to the bottom of the elevator belt – now." I ran but it was too late. A shout and a rumble from the elevator area was followed by howls of laughter. I looked at the bottom of the belt and all I could see was a pile of cereal boxes and a foot protruding beneath them. Lumpkin was shouting to the three female shelf fillers to get him out. We moved the boxes and pulled him to his feet but apart from a bump beginning to show on his forehead, and obviously hurt pride, he was thankfully none the worse. I told him to go to my office and sit down and arranged for someone to bring him some tea. As I gathered the cereal boxes into a pile, my eyes opened wide and my jaw dropped. The idiot had used a Stanley knife to open the whole cases containing cornflakes and the like, and had cut the sides of loads of individual packets, rendering them unsaleable! I really couldn't believe he could have been so stupid.

This episode was the end of the Lumpkin saga at my store. I was at my wits end. The elevator explanation was simple – he hadn't left a gap between the boxes and, after removing the one at the bottom, the landslide of the others followed. What concerned me was that the staff thought so little of him that they simply let it happen.

I couldn't hold on to him. "Take the rest of the day off. Come back tomorrow, and I'll see you in my office to discuss things." He departed. The company did have one store that was very small, busy but uncomplicated and sold only grocery lines. Now, if he went there, surely the Manager, Bill Tubbs – "Tubbsie" – could do something with him. I telephoned the managing director and told him the sad news, which he said was not unexpected. I did, however, suggest "Tubbsie" might be able to do something with him and perhaps he could speak to Bill and see if he'd agree. I felt it would, in the circumstances, be better if the request came from the managing director, and so Mr. Lumpkin arrived at Bill's busy little supermarket in Streatham for the final stage of his brief sojourn in the world of supermarkets.

Bill's store had three checkouts and to his surprise he suddenly had another cashier, because Lumpkin could actually operate a till – and better still – the same kind as Bill had in his old supermarket! Bill's store was old. Had it not been so profitable, the company would have closed it years ago.

There was only room for three tills which were manned most of the time, with Bill himself occasionally taking a turn when occasion required it. That's the way it was and Bill was persuaded by Lumpkin to go home for a bit of lunch and that, if necessary, he'd take his place on the till. Bill replied, he didn't think it would come to that and in any case he'd only be gone for about three quarters of an hour.

He locked the office for safety but gave Lumpkin a spare key in case he needed to get in to use the phone. It was as if poor Lumpkin attracted disaster and bad luck wherever he went because after ten minutes one of the tills broke down. It seized up so with the supermarket down to two tills Lumpkin jumped on the vacant third till, the one Bill would have gone on, hoping to be seen to have taken the initiative. Lumpkin indicated to the long queue on the broken down till to come to him instead. Halfway through his first customer, Lumpkin's own till stopped working! He was panic stricken and dashed to the office which was, of course, locked. He tried the pockets of his overall, then his trousers, but couldn't find the key. "Try your waistcoat pocket for the office key" someone suggested. Fortunately he found the key and then found Bill's telephone number and told him the problem. "Go back to it," yelled Bill … and give the plug point that holds the cables from the till a good kick – now!"

Lumpkin was back on the phone in seconds. "It worked. It worked." "Never mind that. Get back on it – now – and get the queues sorted." Bill returned to the supermarket as quickly as he could and quickly cleared the last of the queues. He then turned his attention to Lumpkin "Have you no sense?" he raged. "Did it not occur to you that the plug might just have come out of the socket? Fancy having to phone me without checking that! And tell me, what did you do with the customer whose shopping you failed to ring up?" "Nothing," replied the hapless Lumpkin. "What could I do? She thumped her basket down and left." Bill groaned. "Why did you not just total her shopping up on a piece of paper and take her money – she wouldn't have minded. Did that not occur to you?" Lumpkin, by report, shook his head wearily.

By all accounts Bill telephoned the managing director and told him he would never put up with anybody who lost him customers and showed so little common sense. Bill was in his late-fifties and took no prisoners but was loyal and dedicated. Perhaps he was harsh but one thing was certain, poor Lumpkin disappeared from any company store, for ever.

Mind you, whilst his performance had been disastrous and a joke, I was well aware of the saying, 'let him without blame cast the first stone'. This is where I come in I'm afraid. I made a mistake that could have been much, much worse than any Lumpkin ever made. Something that would have made big news headlines and something I might never have lived down in my whole life. That serious? Yes, I'm afraid so …

INDEBTED TO ... LEE MARVIN!

I was not an avid autograph hunter but if an opportunity presented itself I'd make the most of it. While I was manager at Golders Green I was also part of the company's football team called Ocean Athletic which played in the London Sunday morning Harlesden League, and was happy to accept the offer from the husband of my chief cashier to drive me to matches and collect me and drive home later.

As we returned after a hot day he wound down his car window to let some fresh air cool us down. Passing Hendon Police Academy the sound of military band music floated into the car. Eric, my driving friend, stopped the car, and, after hearing more music said, "There's no reason why a band should be in there today. What's going on?" We could not see a thing since the walls surrounding the grounds were too high but undaunted he added, "I know how to get in and nobody will see us, so let's have a look. I'm curious."

I followed as he clambered into the grounds where a remarkable scene met our eyes. A film company was in the middle of shooting scenes of a military movie. A quick look around confirmed that and, apart from those concerned with the filming, we were the only intruders. Slowly, and as unobtrusively as possible, we edged our way right up to where the scene was being filmed in front of the main building where rows of soldiers were lined up and being inspected. There was a band present but it was not actually producing music which was coming in stop and start fashion from a tape recorder situated close to me.

Standing next to Eric, surrounded by people involved in filming whom we did not know, I was totally engrossed in the action. As the general once again set out on his inspection to the accompaniment of the music, suddenly I felt a couple of hands on my arm and I was pushed to the side so strongly that, had it not been for Eric, I would have fallen directly onto the tarmac. As I looked up I saw a hydraulic platform on which the camera had descended fairly rapidly, unknown to me, and had it not been for the person who'd pushed me out of the way, I'd have sustained serious head injuries. I hadn't long to find out who it was.

"You alright fella? You gotta watch these things," he said in a rich American voice. "They can be dangerous." I looked round and recognised who'd saved the day – none other than Lee Marvin. As a film buff I'd seen him in *The Caine Mutiny, The Commancheros, Donovan's Reef* and the award-winning *Cat Ballou*.

I learned later this particular film was *The Dirty Dozen*. Needless to say I thanked him sincerely and, when Eric slipped a piece of paper and a pencil to me, asked if he'd mind letting me have his autograph – which he was happy to do. He nodded in the direction of some people off the set and we made our way in that direction. Resting in a hammock reading a paperback western book was Clint Walker, who was well known from the TV *Cheyenne* series. He didn't seem to mind being disturbed and in his rich low American tones responded to a few questions before signing his autograph.

Near him, strumming a guitar, was another personality we recognised. He'd had a number one hit called *If I Had a Hammer* which I had often listened to, and went on to produce more than 30 albums before being inducted into the International Latin Music Hall of Fame in 2003. Trini Lopez was playing the part of Pedro Jiminez in the film and he came across as a warm friendly individual who I later learned had done a great deal of charity work.

The final autograph we managed to obtain was of another actor, Stuart Cooper, although it was much later when I prized his signature, after he directed the superb war film *Operation Overlord*.

We realised we'd been fortunate to have spoken with these stars in such relaxed circumstances and I freely admit when the *Dirty Dozen* gets yet another airing on television the memory of our little escapade brings a smile to my face.

POETRY

At one time I had to drive to reach a couple of the stores I had to manage. Sometimes the journeys could be frustrating and boring, and I used to create poems to match my experiences! I found some of them in a pile of my 'nostalgic rubbish' and thought they might just raise a smile from those who feel they can relate to them!

THE GIRL AT THE PETROL STATION

At my local petrol station there's a girl that's sulky and cheeky and sometimes quite rude.
"Which pump are you?" she always snaps. Her make-up looks so crude!

"What would you do if somebody said,
A pump number that was quite wrong?
And after they'd paid for the wrong bill,
Got away with a full tank for a song?"

"It happens," she said, "Difficult to see the pumps. From this till – the numbers aren't clear."
"Move right", I replied, "and you'll see you can,"
But my advice earned yet another sneer …
"Don't be so clever – I'll do it my way,"
She snarled. Then added with a leer,
"Why don't you ask the garage owners
To make you the manager here!"

"If I did," I thought, "I'd sack you for sure."
Though some might think me a rotter,
Specially the bloke who lives next to me,
Since this brat's his darling daughter!

Going home after a hard long day, temptation to put your foot down on the accelerator pedal is always there, but .....

FOGGY NIGHT, FOGGY MIND

Gosh! The traffic is thick tonight,
Stuck in this slow moving line.
Get home by seven? I'll be lucky.
At this rate it'll be nearly nine.

Hullo! That car way back behind me,
Despite all this fog and rain,
Is darting in and out like mad,
Switching from lane to lane.

Hello! I can see the police ahead,
Checking car speeds once again.
That car behind is now in front!
He's going to get caught – that's plain!

They've pulled him in – what d'you know!
He standing outside his Porsche.
"Have you been drinking?" – they're bound to ask,
– I dream he'll say, "Of corche"!

"Now don't be smug," I say to myself.
Think of your kids and your lovely wife.
Come on! Come on! Cut down your speed
Or your destination's the surgeon's knife!

DELAYED AND DISARMED

As I hurried back to the car park
I glanced up at the town hall clock.
Queuing at the bank, then getting my change.
Bumping into the manager, then talk, talk, talk.

When I finally reached my parking space,
My self-control had finally snapped.
A sleek black MG lay across by bows.
Boxed in? I was bloomin' well trapped.

I got into the car and quietly composed
What to say when the driver re-appears.
My verbal blast will include some words
That I have not used for years!

I suddenly saw the most gorgeous girl.
Best I'd seen for many a day,
Gracefully picking her way through the cars
And most definitely coming my way!

I found myself getting out of the car,
Entranced by her poise and style.
And now – she's standing in front of me
With a coy 'Mona Lisa' smile.

"I know what you must be thinking of me,
But please! Please let me explain.
I'm just back from the chemist, with tablets
For Mum – they're to relieve her pain.

Before I could speak, she spoke again,
"Believe me – I really am sorry .....
I replied, "Don't worry, please be assured
... I wasn't in any great hurry!"

She then drove off smiling and waved goodbye,
Leaving me worrying about my delay.
Then I conjured up thoughts about the girl
Who'd more than brightened my day.

AN UNFORGETTABLE WEEK

In 1963 I was asked by a director to do a holiday relief stint for a week at the Express Dairies supermarket in Wembley. It was a smallish uncomplicated store compared to Harrow which was huge. "I expect you might be bored as there is a lot less to worry about but it's a bit more managerial experience and I hope you do a good job for me!"

The store was basic and the staff showed me the warehouse underneath the sales floor, a cavernous cheerless area with boxes of grocery lines stacked everywhere. I asked where the staff room was but the warehouse manager, a genial middle-aged Irishman, shook his head and said, "Well, the staff sit over there and have their cup of tea." All I could see was a sink, a wooden carton with a kettle and cups on it, and a couple of old stools. "Is that it?" I asked incredulously. "Afraid so," he replied. "Deserve better, don't they?" I snapped.

There and then I resolved to spend my time improving this apology for a staff room. "Have you any building experience?" I asked Tom the Irishman "Oh, yes," he replied, "I used to be in the building trade for a few years."

I had an idea. "Could we – you and I – do something for the staff – put up chipboard walls, shelves for the cups and kettle, and do something with this awful stone floor?" "Yes, we could," he replied. "I know a builder's yard near here where we could buy stuff for next to nothing." "Right," I replied. "I'll get some money from the till and you go and get us organised. I'll do your job and tell the girls what's happening. I'll organise them to run the store while I do your warehouse work and be your building assistant! You'll be the boss. Are you up for it?" He beamed and assured me he was!

He was gold dust. He organised a delivery of three large chipboard walls, wood batons, Marley tiles that were malformed (which he straightened out with his blow-lamp!), nails, screws, etc. We set to and in no time had the walls in place. We both relished the challenge. The sink area was smartened up, shelves were put in place, and Tom did a great job laying the floor tiles! The female staff brought in four old comfy chairs plus crockery and cutlery. To brighten the walls I got some posters from a neighbouring travel agency and strips of plastic hung down as our door. On Saturday morning we celebrated our new staff room! I never before witnessed such a unified effort from an entire store staff.

On Saturday afternoon, the director paid us a visit and when he saw what we'd done he could hardly believe it, especially as the surplus materials had come to less than £10! I asked him privately to thank all the staff, which he did, and went on his way quite happy, I thought. I presented the Irishman with a bottle of malt whisky which I personally paid for because he'd done me proud.

A week later I took a telephone call from the director. "Colin, I was at a meeting this week and put your name forward for assistant manager for our big supermarket in Hounslow. I said you were a good assistant manager and a brilliant builder!"

THE POLICE WERE NOT IMPRESSED

While in a South London supermarket I spotted a lad popping stock from the shelves into the pockets of a three-quarter length, loose fitting coat. As he made his way towards the entrance it was obvious he had been spotted so he raced outside and up the hill. At the time I was especially fit as I played in a competitive Sunday Football League team, so instantly gave chase. He ran and ran but I was confident I'd catch him but soon as he entered a council housing estate he was nowhere to be seen. However, it was December and freezing cold and, on the corner of a building, I noticed hot breath struggling through the frost-bound air.

I approached as quietly and carefully as I could. I sprang round the corner and grabbed him by the lapels. It wasn't difficult as he was doubled up trying to get his breath back. I held on to him and dragged him back on the route I'd taken. After a few yards he started emptying his pockets and was clearly recovering when a police car mounted the pavement right beside me, and two officers made a beeline for the fellow. They yanked him bodily away from me and hurled him into the back of their car where one of the officers sat beside him.

I was told to quickly pick up the stolen items and take the empty front seat, and they then drove back to the police station. I couldn't help reflecting on how uncompromising they'd been in their actions. However, back at the nick they frisked him thoroughly and removed from an inside pocket a lethal looking flick knife with a nine inch blade. I was shocked. One of the officers turned to me, wagged his finger near my nose and hissed, "Now you, look at this." He waved the knife above his head. "Think twice before you go chasing anyone up there again – this is the kind of thing that will put you in hospital or worse – and all for the sake of a few items of stock. Are you listening to what I say?"

"Yes," I replied, adding, "… but it's my stock he's pinching and I've got to stop any shoplifter." Looking at the knife I thought I'd better add, " … see what you mean, though, point taken!" "Meantime," he replied, "we need a statement." This I did, over a mug of tea and a biscuit. Leaving the nick a voice assailed my ears – "Don't forget" – for I was working in an area where crime was an everyday occurrence.

A SAVE IN A MILLION!

At the time the Leicester City and England goalkeeper was Gordon Banks, world class and famous for his acrobatic and spectacular saves but in Camberwell we had his equal in a girl called Linda. She was a pleasant young lady but had a habit of dropping stock on the floor when filling up the shelves. I am a fairly reasonable person but she pushed my patience, especially when filling up the preserves. One morning she dropped and smashed two jars of jam. "Linda," I told her sternly, "... you have to concentrate on what you're doing. You won't have a job filling shelves if you keep dropping stuff on the floor. Do you understand what I'm saying?" She nodded and I could see she was frustrated with herself, poor girl, but there it was. I was not normally cross with staff but her breakages were getting serious.

A little later I came downstairs from the warehouse when I heard a rumble from the area Linda was working in so immediately raced over there. Surely not more breakages.

To this day, however, the image of Linda at this precise moment is still imprinted on my mind. There she was, flat on her back on the cold tiled floor with her right arm fully stretched out holding a jar of strawberry jam – intact. Apparently it had fallen because of vibrations, and Linda had dived and caught it! As she got to her feet she looked at me and said "It wasn't my fault, Mr. MacLeod, it just fell but I knew you wouldn't believe me, so I dived and managed to catch it before it reached the floor!"

I felt humbled. I really did. "Well done." I said to her meaningfully. "Nobody else I know, except perhaps Gordon Banks, could have caught it." I knew then there was no way I would let Linda leave – it was up to me to give her a different section to fill, which I did but that image of her with the jar in her outstretched hand will never leave me.

ROMANCE!

Many people involved in the supermarket industry met their future wives there and I was no exception. Although I made a personal rule never to date any female who worked in the same company store, it did eventually happen, albeit for the shortest of times! I needed an irritating job done on the sales floor involving the baby food section. It had to be re-laid after the shelves had been thoroughly washed but all the stockists were busy and I did not want to interrupt them doing essential work.

I noticed at the tills that Doreen, the chief cashier, was not too busy and since the store was quiet I asked her to make a start. She readily agreed and, when a little later, I had a sly look to see how she was doing, I was very impressed as the area was now sparkling. "My goodness," you have made a good job of cleaning those filthy shelves. I could do with you coming round to my flat and cleaning that up too!" I was caught completely off balance by her response though. "When?" she asked, looking at me straight in the eye. For a moment or two I did not know what to say. She was a very attractive girl, marginally taller than me, and someone

I'd loved to have gone out with on a date but I'd avoided the issue since she worked in the same store. "Well?" she asked meaningfully once again. I felt I could not get out of this, and in truth did not want to pass up the chance. Stutteringly, I said, "Well, next Wednesday evening – if you come round to my flat we can have a meal there and talk, and then go out somewhere If you'd like to." "Right," she said, "See you around say 7.15 pm. OK?"

So there it was, my first date with Doreen. I was no cook and my Scottish architect flatmate was on holiday, so it would have to be two Birds Eye Dinner meals for one. Pop the contents in the oven and just heat it up. There was a can of peaches in the larder plus Carnation cream so that would do for dessert! Big deal! At this time I was hopeless at cooking!

On the Wednesday evening the manager had, without warning, decided to work late. Well, I use the word inaccurately because he was lazy and had given me a task I was going to be lucky to finish and get home in time for my date. I finished the work, checked the time, and then said to him, "I've got to leave now because I have someone coming to my flat. Can you take the money for the two Birds Eye dinners?" He went to the freezer and took two out.

He was, however, an uncouth person and decided to make a big thing of my simple request. When I asked how much they were I thought they were overpriced and remarked rather foolishly about it. As a manager he was an embarrassment and shouted out loud, "My assistant manager" grudges paying the price for two dinners for one and he's entertaining a bird at his flat!" (he guessed this). Everybody had a laugh, especially when he added a few extras about the date and what my intentions would be.

I was both embarrassed and angry, took my leave and raced back to my flat where I left the dinner by the cooker, while I made my way to the bathroom to wash and shave. I heard the front door ring and mistakenly thought it was the "the man from the Pru" to collect his money but it wasn't. Standing there with shaving soap on my face and wearing my vest and trousers, I found myself facing my date. She looked great but was nearly half an hour early! She'd fortuitously caught the earlier bus and there she was! I left her in the living room but, by the time I'd finished shaving, washing and putting on a clean shirt and tie, the dinner was nearly ready to be served! Not only had she laid the table, she'd cooked the meal as well! Some first date!

We later went for a drink and agreed we'd keep this and future dates quiet but that one of us would have to find different employment, which we felt was the only way.

Next day I was in the office with the manager who, when he saw Doreen – who was to become my future wife – he regaled her with the "dinner for one" saga and how mean I was. I noticed Doreen's face flush. "It wasn't you, was it?" said the manager suddenly. "It most certainly was not!" was Doreen's angry reply. "I would not go out with anyone so mean – never." The manager tried to apologise but she stormed off. It transpired she had already applied for, and got, a chief cashier's position with the bigger Tesco supermarket near us, where she was also to be better paid.

Did she really think I was mean? The answer is a resounding "No!" We enjoyed going out together for some time until we eventually got married, by which time I'd left the store for another one and was later promoted to manager. Happy days!

THE WORST WEEK OF MY LIFE

My area manager interviewed a girl for the vacant cashier/ clerk position at the Didcot supermarket, where I was manager. I'd only just taken up the position and did not yet know the staff very well. It was a Friday night and all the money from the tills had been counted which I inserted into the bank wallets, watched by the new cashier. It was close to 8pm as we closed for business and I was pushing the final notes into the last wallet, when there was a knock on the office door, which was of course locked and with an additional chain lock.

I opened the door cautiously and a customer said "Could you just show me where the water biscuits are – if you stock them – there's nobody to ask." Since they were a few paces from the office and all seemed safe, after first shutting the office door I walked over to them.

Seconds later, having helped the customer, I was back in the office where the new cashier was pushing the notes into the wallet on the desk where I'd left it before I was interrupted. I then took the short walk across the road and popped the wallets into the safe keeping of the bank's night safe. However, on the following Monday I received a call from the bank telling me one of the wallets was £200 short! Having counted the cash myself I thought the mistake must be the bank's but it was quickly proven the money had not been in the wallet and I had been the last to handle it, after watching the clerk struggle to close it before me.

I had just taken out a mortgage for a house in Didcot while my family were staying in London so this was the last thing I wanted. For a whole week the local CID interviewed me at length, until I decided enough was enough and that I would have to resign.

It was after the store was shut and I was alone in the office – all the staff had gone home – when a CID officer knocked on the shop window wanting to speak to me. "You," he said, "have given everyone in here alibis why they could not possibly have stolen the cash, leaving yourself as prime suspect. Do you realise that? Now I want you to very slowly tell me in minute detail how things were in the office when you say you put the money into the wallet." I really did not want to go over it again but he insisted. However, this time I had included what I had not mentioned before – the incident involving the customer and her request and the fact that I had left the office, albeit for a very short time. And, "No – I had not re-checked to see that the amount in the wallet (already counted) was still the same."

"Now we are getting somewhere," said the CID man, and seemed very pleased with himself. No wonder. Within hours the new cashier was taken to the police station and interviewed. I was later told "She was probably the coolest and calmest person we'd interviewed in years but in the end we got her. Did you know she took a taxi home that night though she was in digs 200 yards away? Well, she did and she could afford it! She eventually confessed to taking the money in the few seconds you left the office and thought it was impossible to take it and hide it. We knew you hadn't taken it but it was hard to get the full story." He smiled and patted me on the back, then added, "Your head office told us that it was definitely not you who was the culprit, and to keep looking – which we did!".

I was grateful to him but it had still been the worst week of my life!

NEWS 'N' STANDARD' SELLER

I hadn't been working in London for long and was just finding my feet. At the end of a long day as assistant manager at Hounslow, I was standing outside a wet and windy Osterley Tube station waiting impatiently for a colleague to arrive before setting off for an old First Division football match (now the Premier League), when the chap standing beside his evening paper stand decided he needed to attend to a call of nature, and promptly disappeared.

Whilst staring down the road, somebody tapped my arm and thrust a coin into my hand and picked up a newspaper. Before I could react, another bloke did the same! I now realised the old raincoat I was wearing to prevent me getting soaked had to go. Clearly it was well out of fashion and I was not an impoverished newspaper vendor which some folk clearly thought I was!

Next day I purchased a smart dark blue modern shortie raincoat and felt like a new person. I still wince when I think how slow I'd been to realise I was living and working in London during the Swinging Sixties!

THE GRAPEVINE WORKED

The grapevine is very effective when spread by local shopkeepers trying to minimise theft.

"Watch for a guy with an extra long overcoat" said the voice on the telephone. "He'll wander aimlessly around and then dart into a spot not covered by security. We couldn't trap him but we are certain he's putting things into his large coat pockets. We're sure he's at it and if it's raining he'll have an umbrella as well, a longish handled one. We wouldn't be surprised if he puts stuff in there as well!"

I alerted the staff, and a couple of weeks later an eagle-eyed member of staff spotted him and was smart enough to observe him putting small expensive cosmetic lines into his pocket. He did it twice so we nabbed him outside the store and called the police.

I explained to them we'd had a tip-off and that he'd done thieving elsewhere, and although they'd not been in a position to catch him they had tipped us off. Both myself and the police officer complimented the young girl on her alertness, and we both wished there were more like her. I also telephoned the grapevine caller to thank him, who was understandably delighted the thief had been caught and apprehended.

ALLEZ-VOUS-EN!

A local store manager warned me about a bunch of French youngsters who had come into his store unnoticed, until they were spotted crowding around the confectionery section rifling the sweets! They were soon ushered out but with some difficulty.

That particular morning I spotted them as they entered my store and made their way to the confectionery section just as I had been warned. They quickly formed a ring around the shelves to start stealing but I was ready for them. I recalled the French for "go away!" and approached them quietly before bellowing at the top of my voice, "Allez-vous-en! Allez-vous-en!", waving my arms accentuating what I was shouting. Half a dozen alarmed faces turned to stare at me with a mixture of fear and apprehension and were off without argument. My staff were impressed and assured me they would keep an eye open for them in the future. Happily, they never returned.

Local language difficulties

I had been working in my supermarket in the north east of Scotland for only a few days before my lack of knowledge of the local dialect reared its head! A lady came in and said "I cannot find the butteries". Trouble was I thought she meant batteries and pointed to the shelves they were on. She looked puzzled and so I said, "On the end of the shelf". She was now doubly puzzled so I went over to help her. When I pointed to them she simply roared with laughter and explained that what she wanted were like morning rolls and were called "butteries"! Other staff members also had a real giggle and I couldn't blame them! I really had to learn the local dialect!

A local farmer came up to me a couple of days later and asked for what I thought were towels so I returned with a couple of different ones to show him. "Oh aye," he said, "I see you don't understand – what I want is towies or towel – rope, rope!" We had a good laugh together as I found him what he wanted.

AN INSIDE STORY!

In order to protect a supermarket from being robbed, I learned from first hand experience that security officers sometimes have to bend the rules to get the results they are paid to achieve. At one London store my chief cashier was certain that one of the other cashiers was dishonest. There are ways to extract money from tills without it being apparent and it can be quite tricky to identify and stop it before some real damage is done. The lady in question had a boyfriend who used to live with her but for some reason had returned to his native Ireland.

Her demeanour was not a happy one and disconcerting whispers began circulating so we had a private chat with the company's security officer who paid us a visit. Whilst he was in our office the post arrived among which he discovered a letter addressed "c/o" our store to the cashier about whom we had our suspicions. The security officer examined the postmark very carefully and announced the letter had been posted in Ireland. He was ex-CID and we witnessed something we never thought was possible.

Carefully and very slowly, he inserted a pencil into a corner of the back the envelope and gently rolled it round until the envelope opened enough for him to see inside, then extracted the letter. We watched his eyebrows lift and knew it contained something of interest, the contents telling him that the cashier had been giving the sender money but also that his letters to her address were now remaining unanswered, hence the letter addressed to the store. Apparently the sender was demanding more money, or else he was going to inform the source via an anonymous letter – a case of a loving relationship turning sour.

It was a nasty blackmail letter which we left to the CID to sort out. I have since tried to open letters like the security officer but have never succeeded.

LAST CHANCE SALOON AT WINDSOR

Some folk enjoy a flutter on a horse and I have a quiet laugh when I remember the time my butcher and assistant manager in Didcot went to watch an evening's racing at Windsor. They lost on every race they backed and as the twilight descended were leaning over the rail at the side of the track in despair, when a big horse appeared through the gloom making its way from the paddock to the start. Aware there was nobody near them, the butcher called over to the jockey and mentioned they had had a bad night and did the jockey think his horse might win. He didn't think he'd get a reply but the horse was quite near and to their surprise the jockey looked at them and gave them a clear knowing wink and nod of his head.

They rushed to find a bookie and put all they had left on the horse in a final effort to overcome their losses. It won and next day they regaled the story of how they'd gone from a horrible loss to a significant profit. I hoped they had learned a lesson but betting can be a dangerous activity.

BE SURE YOU KNOW WHO
YOU'RE SPEAKING TO

Joyce, a conscientious assistant, was working one evening on the shelves below the counter completely unseen when, quite by chance, a young male customer strolled up to the counter with his mobile phone in hand. He had just contacted his girlfriend and the subsequent conversation began with his greeting "Hello darling, how are you today?" Joyce, quite unaware of the situation taking place, replied in all innocence, "Oh, not too bad thanks". The young chap continued, "Good – and what are you up to today?" With seemingly no prospect of him being served, however, the chap moved away, just as Joyce reappeared feeling profoundly foolish for unwittingly chipping into someone else's phone call!

Something similar once happened to me when I'd been asked to cover the management of the Dover store, many miles from my where I lived. Staying overnight in an hotel I decided to telephone my wife from one of two phone kiosks outside. I heard her answer and, despite a poor line, rattled on for a few minutes without waiting for her response. When it came, it was a different voice, "I'm sorry, but I'm afraid you have the wrong number!" "Oh, I'm so sorry!" I replied, apologising for my gaffe. However, I need not have worried because her response was, "Don't apologise. I was sitting here all on my own feeling quite miserable and glum and you've cheered me up – thank you!"

When I re-joined a friend at the hotel and told him the story, he shook his head and said, "Why didn't you get her address and go over there to cheer her up a bit more

A PAIN IN THE NECK

My area manager once made an early call to the super-market at Didcot, wanting to make an immediate inspection of the sales floor. I was quite happy and ready for him but noticed his face grimaced with pain after only a few steps so I asked if there was anything wrong. "Yes. It's coming from the back of my neck and is sore and most uncomfortable." Although he was quite a bit taller than me, I asked if I could take a look, to which he readily agreed.

I pulled back the lapel of his jacket and could see the problem. Making the most of it I asked him to keep still to see if I could alleviate his difficulty. This I did and he immediately expressed his delight. "How did you do it?" "Well, I noticed you were wearing a drip dry nylon shirt which are easy to wash but in future be careful to leave this on the washing line, not on your shirt."

I then held up a clothes peg which had been the cause of his painful experience. "You know," he said, shaking his head, "I grabbed it off the line this morning in a hurry and never noticed the peg was still attached! Thanks a lot!".

"Well", I replied, "Instead of walking round the store – which is fine by the way – why don't we celebrate with a nice cup of tea and a morning roll in my office?" He laughed and readily agreed, his relief being very apparent!

A FOOTBALLING MISHAP

As assistant manager at Premier's large Hounslow super-market, I was fortunate to have help from a bright trainee called Austen. We made a good team and both of us were keen footballers. Early one morning I checked out the store's fresh fish counter. Halfway down the aisle in front of the counter I noticed a dried up round fish lying there which resembled a football. Austen appeared by chance at the opposite end of the aisle so I shouted, "Race you to the ball". We both sprinted immediately towards it. A split second before his foot reached the object my foot connected with it first. Unfortunately he was wearing slip-on shoes and after booting thin air, his shoe flew up landing on the large mirror-glass fish mural on the wall behind the fish counter smashing it to smithereens.

"Quick, Austen", I shouted to him. "Get your shoe and start sweeping up right now!"

A couple of staff appeared to see what had happened, so I told them what I later said to the Manager: "Austen was sweeping behind the counter when the end of his broom went through the glass. Pure accident!" The store's insurance covered the cost, and by agreement Austen and I never talked about it. Both of us had learned a lesson – and, to be honest, this is the first time I have ever come clean!

Well, we don't live in a perfect world, do we?

Come to think about it …

After reading all the stories and confessions in this account of supermarket life, I am sure this is something you, the reader, will heartily agree with!

COLIN S MACLEOD

Born in Aberdeen, Colin MacLeod spent his childhood in Turriff and Fyvie, after following a fourth year Higher education course at Inverurie Academy, in 1957 he left to become Assistant Manager at Coopers (Finefare) Supermarket in Northfield, Aberdeen.

He came top in Scotland in repeated years in the Institute of Certificated Grocers national exams, headhunted, he joined Premier Supermarkets (part of Express Dairies) in London. He remained in supermarket management for forty years.

For thirty years he also wrote professionally and regularly for four magazines. In 1991, following an appearance on BBC Radio 4 Poetry Please, he produced a book called *Hoots Mon!* containing humorous Scottish poems which was hugely successful.

He has since written four books, one of which resides in the Strathmartine Archaeological Library in Edinburgh. He has two daughters, Helen and Sarah, and a son, Roy. Widowed, he now lives with his partner Angela in Beauly, Scotland.